Do-It-Yourself Decorating

Step-by-Step
Interior Painting

Julian Cassell & Peter Parham

Meredith® Press

Des Moines, Iowa

Contents

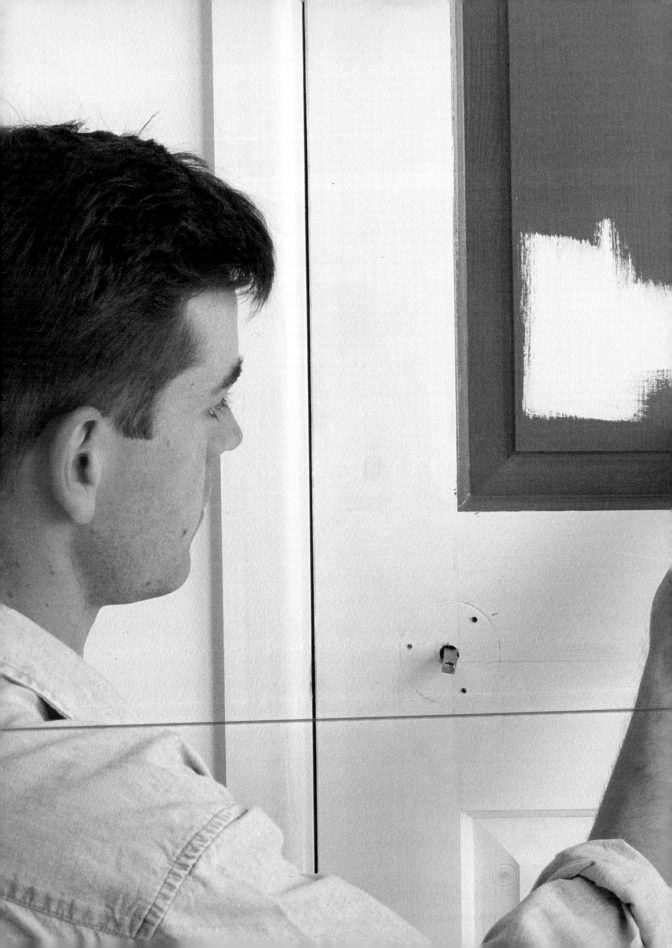

Introduction

Whether you're a beginner or someone who has done lots of painting, this book will tell you how to paint every room in your house.

There's such a wide variety of paints and finishes on the market that it can be hard to choose. Start with the "Ideas and Choices" chapter for help in picking the right products for your project. It has suggestions and ideas for all sorts of color schemes—from neutrals on walls to bold colors on woodwork.

It's very important to plan your work and to take the time to perform all of the steps in the order that makes the most sense. The "Planning and Preparation" chapter will help you do just that, making sure you don't leave out any necessary steps.

The use of lining paper is often considered optional by many painters and decorators. Although lining the walls and/or ceilings takes extra time, it provides a flatter, more even surface for painting, especially on old lath-and-plaster surfaces.

The "Painting" chapter will teach the basics to beginners and improve the technique of more experienced painters. Again, ideas and options are presented to provide the widest possible range of choices for all aspects of painting.

Good luck with all of your interior painting projects. By following the steps in this book, you'll achieve both the look you want and the quality of finish that your hard work deserves.

Ideas and Choices

Often, the hardest part of painting is choosing your colors and finishes. Many people lose sleep worrying about precisely matching the walls, ceiling, and woodwork with particular furnishings or fabrics. If this has been your experience in the past, just remember that redecorating a room should be fun, not a chore.

Your inspiration may not come immediately, so use all available resources to help with your decision-making. Most paint manufacturers provide color swatches to help you experiment.

It may be helpful to find rooms or styles that have caught your eye in magazines. Above all, remember that your personal taste and preferences are what matters most.

This chapter doesn't attempt to push rigid guidelines but provides you with options to consider when selecting color schemes and the types of paint that are available to make them look their best.

Pale colors

Colors that are neutral and pale always give an impression of space because they reflect light more than darker colors. Rooms that don't get much natural light look airier when they have pale walls and ceilings, and some rooms may look less cluttered than they really are.

The most common application of this principle is when ceilings are painted white to increase the apparent height of a room.

Pale colors also tend to be popular, because it's easier to match furnishings with neutral tones than it is with bolder, more vibrant ones.

◀ Pastel colors tend to be calming and to produce a relaxed, comfortable atmosphere. Shades of peach and apricot add warmth to this room. The pale slate blue provides a nice contrast, but because it's of similar intensity to the wall color, the overall effect is still restful.

◄ Pale colors are the perfect backdrop for favorite furnishings, accessories, and displays.

▲ Bright yellow, although not a neutral color, adds life to what might otherwise be a dull area. Other primary colors have a similar effect in lifting the apparent mood of a room.

◄ Greens and blues are considered cool colors, providing a fresh, soothing atmosphere. The lighter the shade, the more the walls will tend to recede, giving the impression of space. In addition, pictures and paintings stand out better against a light background.

Dark colors

Dark colors are always a bold choice: They add considerable character to flat, lifeless surfaces and accentuate the features of a room. Dark colors may create a slightly enclosed feeling, appearing to bring high ceilings down and making walls advance rather than recede. You can use this effect to create a cozy, relaxed feeling, especially in rooms used primarily in the evening.

If dark colors seem a bit too daring, use them on woodwork instead, where they won't be as overpowering as they'd be on a large wall surface. Remember, it's often best to use a color one or two shades lighter than your original choice; a color always seems darker after you apply it, especially on large areas.

▲ The deep brick red on the back walls complements the green shelves and creates an added decorating dimension.

◀ The dark forest green of this woodwork stands out against the pale yellow walls, emphasizing the shape of the bookshelves and providing an ideal showcase for collectibles, books, and just about any kind of display you can imagine.

◄ Dark blues are cool colors that often can provide the perfect touch of relaxation.

▼ Lighting changes the appearance of colors dramatically. The blue on these walls fairly shimmers with the glow from the nearby lamp.

◄ Rich, dark red enhances the natural beauty of wood and adds a certain opulence to soft furnishings. By keeping the window bay white, the natural light that enters the room is maximized.

Paint finishes

Almost all interior paints can be divided into two broad categories: water-based and solvent-based.

Water-based paints have gained in popularity, mainly because they're easy to use and are environmentally friendly. Solvent-based paints, although traditionally considered more durable than water-based paints, aren't as user-friendly.

	PRODUCT	SURFACES
PRIMER	Watery, dilute appearance specifically formulated to seal bare surfaces.	All bare wood, plaster, and metal. Use specific primer for each surface. All-purpose primers are available.
PRIMER-UNDERCOAT	A primer and undercoat in one, providing base for top coat(s).	Bare wood.
UNDERCOAT	Dull, opaque finish providing ideal base for top coat(s).	Any primed surface.
FLAT WATER-BASED	All purpose flat-finish paint.	Plaster surfaces.
URETHANE PAINT	Plastic-based, pigmented variations of polyurethane varnishes. Usually oil-based.	Almost any porous surface or existing finish.
SEMIGLOSS WATER-BASED	Mid-sheen finish paint.	Any primed or undercoated surface.
GLOSS WATER-BASED	Shiny finish paint.	Any undercoated surface, ideally wood or metal.
TEXTURED PAINT	Textured paint that can be used as a finish or painted over.	Plaster surfaces.
FLOOR PAINT	Finish paint for floors.	Ideal for concrete. Can be used on brick, cement, wood, and stone.
VARNISH	Translucent natural-wood finish available in gloss, semigloss, and flat finishes.	All bare wood. May be applied over most previously stained surfaces. Water-based is excellent for floors.
STAIN	Deep, penetrating natural-wood finish. Variety of sheens available.	All bare wood. Darker colors may be applied over previously stained surfaces.
WAX	A natural finish for wood.	All bare wood. Some waxes may require sealing the wood before application.
OIL	Penetrating natural-wood treatment.	All bare wood, although hardwoods such as oak and ash produce the best finishes.

Besides these, there are some special paints that require specific preparation and application techniques. Remember to pay attention to the manufacturer's instructions. The chart below gives you all the information you'll need about the most common paint and wood finishes available today, both water- and solvent-based.

Always read the manufacturer's instructions for each product. There may be small variations in the categories outlined in the chart.

PROS	CONS	APPLICATION
Excellent sealer.	Only use on bare surfaces.	Brush. May use roller or spray with water-based primers.
Quick and easy to use.	Not as hard-wearing as oil-based undercoat.	Brush, roller, or spray.
Hard-wearing.	Application takes longer than primer-undercoat.	Brush or roller.
A thinned top coat is an excellent primer. Subsequent undiluted coats can be applied for finishing.	Not hard-wearing.	Brush, roller, or spray.
Very durable and resistant to grease, dirt, and abrasion.	Can be costly and tricky to apply.	Brush or roller.
Hard-wearing.	Slight sheen tends to accentuate imperfections on large surfaces.	Brush, roller, or spray.
Very hard-wearing finish. Easy to clean.	Application takes longer than most other paints, and special care is needed for good results.	Brush or roller.
Adds dimension to flat walls or ceilings. Excellent for hiding rough surfaces.	Difficult to clean textured wall surfaces. Difficult to remove when redecorating.	Roller, brush, combs/variety of finishing tools.
Hard-wearing finish for floors. Easy to clean.	Color choice limited. Use on floors only. New concrete may require curing for up to 6 months before painting.	Brush or roller.
Very hard-wearing, durable, and easy to clean.	Solvent-based yellows with age.	Brush, roller, or spray.
Hard-wearing. Enhances the grain and features of natural wood.	Difficult to strip or change color once applied, so choose your colors carefully.	Brush.
Accentuates natural beauty of wood; depth and quality of finish improves over time with more applications.	Regular applications needed to maintain finish.	Brush and/or cloth. Cloth for buffing.
Can be used mainly as a preservative or to provide a polished finish.	Regular applications needed. Extra care needed when cleaning up because some are combustible.	Brush and/or cloth. Cloth for removing excess.

Order of work

It's important to work in the right order when you get ready to apply your chosen finish. The illustrations below show the products you'll need for each finish and the order in which they should be applied. Remember that skipping a step will almost inevitably give you a final finish that's inferior to what you'd otherwise have achieved.

WATER-BASED PAINT ON NEW PLASTER

1 Bare plaster
2 Dilute flat water-based primer coat
3 First coat of finish paint
4 Top coat of finish paint (apply further coats if required)

WATER-BASED PAINT ON LINING PAPER

1 Bare plaster
2 Sealer or size
3 Lining paper
4 Finish paint: two or three coats

WATER-BASED vs. SOLVENT-BASED: THE PROS AND CONS

	WATER-BASED	SOLVENT-BASED	COMMENTS
EASE OF APPLICATION	• • • • •	• • •	Water-based tends to be easier to apply, with less brushing out required.
DRYING TIME	• • • • •	•	Much quicker drying between coats with water-based paints.
ODOR	• • • • •	•	The smell of solvent-based paints can be overpowering. Minimal problem with water-based.
WASHABILITY	• • •	• • • • •	Surfaces painted with solvent-based paints are easiest to clean.
DURABILITY	• • •	• • • • •	Solvent-based are more hard-wearing, although water-based are catching up with improved formulations.
BRUSH MARKS	• •	• • • •	More evident in water-based, although improving all the time.
COLOR RETENTION	• • • •	• • •	White solvent-based (especially) tends to yellow with age.
CLEANING TOOLS	• • • • •	•	Water-based is easily cleaned with water and mild detergent. Solvent-based is more difficult.
SAFETY	• • • •	•	Health and safety guidelines may make water-based products a better choice than their solvent-based counterparts.

WATER-BASED PAINT ON WOOD

1 Bare wood
2 Sealer on bare knots
3 Primer-undercoat
4 Second primer-undercoat for improved finish (or apply first coat of semigloss paint if top coat is going to be semigloss)
5 Top coat: gloss or semigloss paint

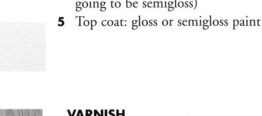

OIL-BASED PAINT ON WOOD

1 Bare wood
2 Sealer on bare knots
3 Primer
4 Undercoat: two coats for improved finish
5 Top coat: gloss (if using semigloss paint, two coats directly on top of primer; undercoat not necessary)

VARNISH

1 Bare wood
2 Wood stain: optional, to color wood
3 Varnish: two coats if water-based (thinned primer coat and at least two top coats required if solvent-based)

WAX

1 Bare wood
2 Wood stain: optional, to color wood
3a Light-colored wax: two coats for finishing, or
3b Darker wax: two coats for finishing

STAIN

1 Bare wood
2 First coat of stain (proprietary primer coat may be required)
3 Second coat of stain
4 Third coat of stain, depending on shade and depth of color required

OIL

1 Bare wood
2 First coat of oil
3 Second coat of oil (apply additional coats depending on absorption of wood)

Planning and Preparation

Successful painting depends on careful planning and thorough preparation. You need to make decisions about what the particular job requires and how to go about it. Being methodical at this early stage will save you time later on. Halfway through a job, no one likes to run out of paint or discover they don't have the right tools. Surface preparation is key; it's the initial hard work and not the application of the finish coat that determines the results you get. Even though modern-day materials are better than ever, your results are bound to be disappointing if your surface preparation is poor.

Tools

When choosing and buying tools and equipment, always remember to go for quality over quantity. A few well-chosen quality items will be much more useful than cheap "all-in-one" tool kits that often include items you'll never use.

When assembling your tools, don't feel you have to go out and buy everything you see here. Instead, buy just for your specific, immediate needs, and build up your set of equipment gradually. Also, if you'll have limited use for an item, especially if it's an expensive one such as a steam stripper, it may make more sense to rent it rather than buy it.

BASIC PREPARATION TOOLS

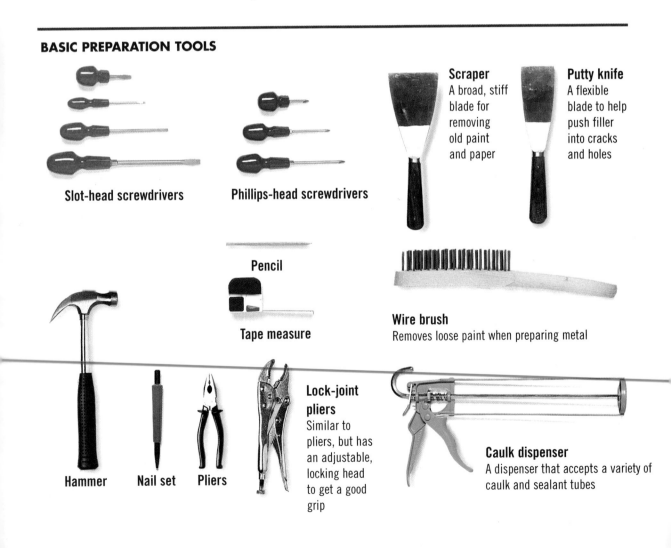

Slot-head screwdrivers

Phillips-head screwdrivers

Scraper
A broad, stiff blade for removing old paint and paper

Putty knife
A flexible blade to help push filler into cracks and holes

Pencil

Tape measure

Wire brush
Removes loose paint when preparing metal

Hammer

Nail set

Pliers

Lock-joint pliers
Similar to pliers, but has an adjustable, locking head to get a good grip

Caulk dispenser
A dispenser that accepts a variety of caulk and sealant tubes

Access and protection

Stepladder

Drop cloth

Sawhorses and boards
Make a sturdy platform when working on ceilings or high walls

Personal protection

Protective gloves
Waterproof, to keep irritants off hands

Goggles
Keep dust, spray, and chemicals out of eyes

Dust masks
(disposable)

Respirator mask
Protects against fine dust and fumes

Stripping and sanding

Electric sander
For large areas

Electric hot-air gun
For stripping paint or varnish

Steam stripper
For fast wallpaper stripping

WALLPAPERING TOOLS

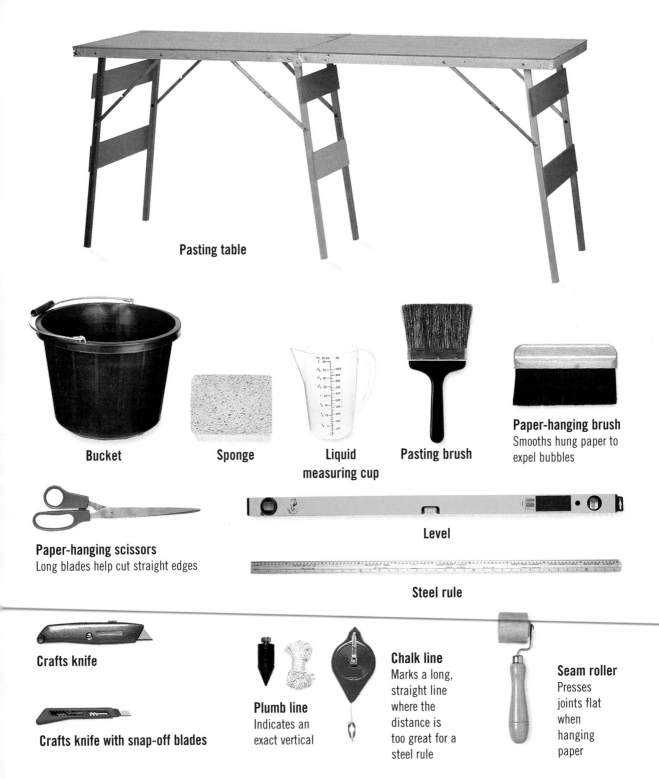

Pasting table

Bucket

Sponge

Liquid measuring cup

Pasting brush

Paper-hanging brush
Smooths hung paper to expel bubbles

Paper-hanging scissors
Long blades help cut straight edges

Level

Steel rule

Crafts knife

Crafts knife with snap-off blades

Plumb line
Indicates an exact vertical

Chalk line
Marks a long, straight line where the distance is too great for a steel rule

Seam roller
Presses joints flat when hanging paper

PAINTING TOOLS
Preparation

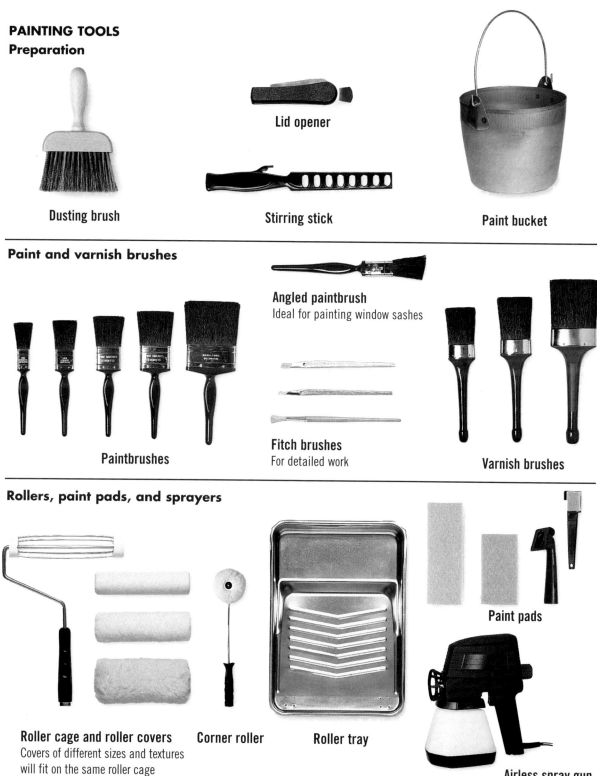

Dusting brush

Lid opener

Stirring stick

Paint bucket

Paint and varnish brushes

Angled paintbrush
Ideal for painting window sashes

Paintbrushes

Fitch brushes
For detailed work

Varnish brushes

Rollers, paint pads, and sprayers

Paint pads

Roller cage and roller covers
Covers of different sizes and textures
will fit on the same roller cage

Corner roller

Roller tray

Airless spray gun

Identifying problems

Before starting any of the actual painting you've planned, you first need to clear the room of all furnishings and obstructions. It's best to remove everything you can carry, then to take up any rugs and protect carpeting at this stage. If it's not going to be possible to totally clear the room, then move everything to the center and cover it with drop cloths. This way you can get a better idea of where problem areas might be and how you're going to handle them. The problems shown here are common in many homes, and all of them need attention before you start to paint.

MOISTURE AND MOLD

Mold is caused by moisture buildup, usually as a result of poor ventilation. Wash the area thoroughly with fungicide. Extensive mold growth should be looked at by a professional, because there may be an underlying moisture problem that needs to be corrected before painting takes place. Cover old moisture stains that have dried out with a commercial sealer.

CRACKED/CHIPPED WOODWORK

Results from general wear and tear. Depending on the damage, the woodwork may need to be stripped or just filled and sanded before it's repainted (see pages 34–35).

WRINKLED PAPER

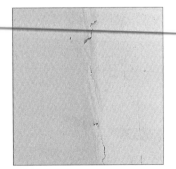

Commonly found in corners where the walls aren't quite square or where there was poor paper adhesion or slight settling in the building. To make repairs, cut out small areas with a scraper, then apply patches and paint over them.

BLEEDING KNOTS

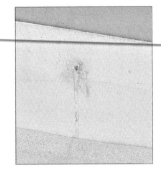

Caused by resin weeping from a live knot, usually in relatively new wood. Strip the wood and seal (see pages 28–29).

POWDERY WALL SURFACES

This condition is more common in older homes with lath-and-plaster walls and ceilings, and is caused by the breakdown of old plaster. Wash the area and seal (see pages 36–37).

FLAKING TEXTURED FINISHES

Caused by water penetration (such as a broken pipe) or a poorly prepared surface. Small areas can be patched. With larger areas, the whole surface must be stripped and the finish reapplied.

FLAKY PAINT

Caused by moisture underneath the painted surface, or where the paint has been unable to stick to a powdery or incompatible surface (see left, and Sealing on pages 36–37).

UNEVEN PAPERED SURFACES

This problem generally is found in older homes. If the paper is basically sound or an overall "rustic" look is what you're after, do not strip the paper; the plaster underneath may come away from the wall.

EFFLORESCENCE

Results from the crystallization of salts found in some building materials. Use a scraper to remove deposits until no more appear. Repaint with water-based paint, which allows drying to continue through the painted surface.

LIFTING WALLPAPER SEAMS

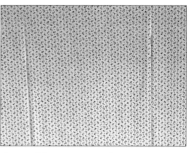

Caused by poor application, lack of paste adhesion due to moisture, or simply age. Stick small areas of lining paper back down with border adhesive. With larger areas, the whole room should be stripped and repapered.

BUBBLING PAPER

This is caused by sloppy papering or poor adhesion. The only solution is to strip and repaper the problem area (see pages 26–27).

CRACKS IN PLASTER

Caused by drying out, building settlement, and general wear and tear. Fill and let dry completely before painting or papering (see pages 30–31).

Paints and materials

When buying materials—and especially paint—spend a little more on quality products to save you both time and money in the long run. It's penny wise and pound foolish to apply four or five coats of a cheap paint when a slightly more expensive product would have done the job in two coats. And don't buy more paint than you can use right away; some paints and finishes have a limited shelf life and don't store well.

BASIC SUPPLIES
Fillers

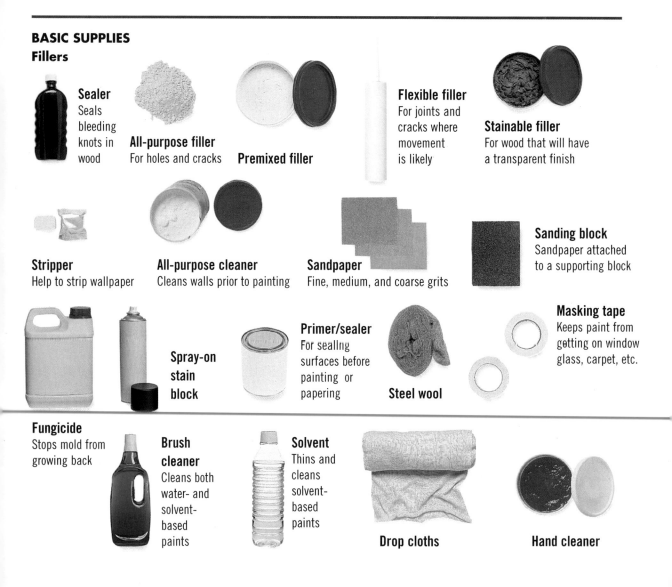

Sealer
Seals bleeding knots in wood

All-purpose filler
For holes and cracks

Premixed filler

Flexible filler
For joints and cracks where movement is likely

Stainable filler
For wood that will have a transparent finish

Stripper
Help to strip wallpaper

All-purpose cleaner
Cleans walls prior to painting

Sandpaper
Fine, medium, and coarse grits

Sanding block
Sandpaper attached to a supporting block

Spray-on stain block

Primer/sealer
For sealing surfaces before painting or papering

Steel wool

Masking tape
Keeps paint from getting on window glass, carpet, etc.

Fungicide
Stops mold from growing back

Brush cleaner
Cleans both water- and solvent-based paints

Solvent
Thins and cleans solvent-based paints

Drop cloths

Hand cleaner

LINING

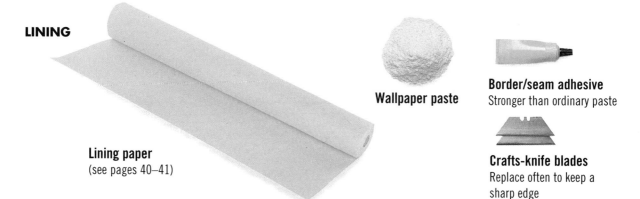

Lining paper
(see pages 40–41)

Wallpaper paste

Border/seam adhesive
Stronger than ordinary paste

Crafts-knife blades
Replace often to keep a
sharp edge

FINISHING

Primer
Undercoat
Top coat: flat,
semigloss,
or gloss

Stain
Varnish
Wax
Oil
Wood stain

CAUTION
Some materials contain hazardous chemicals. Always remember to read the manufacturer's instructions before handling them.

COVERAGE

To estimate quantities, you first need to measure all surface areas. Walls and ceilings are relatively easy; you can use the same method used to measure for lining paper (see pages 40–41).

When calculating how much paint you need for a window, measure it as if it were a door by multiplying the height by the width. Don't deduct for the glass area; this will compensate for the intricate areas of the window that make its actual surface area larger than it would appear. (However, do make a deduction for the glass areas of picture windows.)

The table at right is just an approximate guide to how much paint you'll need; some surfaces are more porous than others. These figures were calculated for surfaces of average porosity. Each manufacturer's paints will produce slight variations in coverage, so it's best also to take their estimates into account when planning how much to buy.

ACRYLIC/WATER-BASED

	sq. yd./gallon
Gloss	82
Semigloss	82
Water-based	82
Primer/undercoat	65
Varnish	55

SOLVENT/OIL-BASED

Gloss	92
Semigloss	87
Undercoat	82
Primer	71
Varnish	82
Wood stain	120

Stripping paper

This is a time-consuming job, but if you follow these steps, it's a relatively easy one. A steam stripper, which you can rent inexpensively, speeds things up considerably. When using it, always wear rubber gloves and goggles; boiling water and steam can spit out of the sides of the stripping pad and cause burns. If a steam stripper isn't available, soak the paper with hot water or use a stripper solution instead. You'll still need gloves and goggles, though, because most chemical strippers will irritate the skin.

TOOLS: Gloves, goggles, steam stripper, liquid measuring cup, scraper, bucket, stirring stick, 5-inch brush, wallpaper perforator

MATERIALS: Stripper, water

STEAM-STRIPPING

1 When using a steam stripper, always read the instructions. Check that the power to the machine is off, then pour water into its reservoir. Warm water will reduce the time needed for the stripper to boil. Then switch on the power and wait for the water to boil. And remember—never leave a steam stripper unattended when it's running.

2 Put on your goggles and gloves. Place the stripper's steam pad firmly on the wallpaper you want to strip, holding it in the same position without moving it for about 30 seconds. Some brands of wallpaper stripper and some heavy papers may need a longer steaming time.

3 Move the pad across the wall and, using a scraper, strip off the loose, bubbling paper. Be careful not to dig the end of the scraper into the wall, gouging holes in the plaster. You'll soon develop a rhythm of stripping the paper with one hand while steaming the next section of wall with the other.

STRIPPING WITH WATER

1 Measure the hot water into a bucket and add the correct amount of wallpaper stripper. Stir thoroughly until the stripper is completely dissolved. Hot water alone also will work for soaking wallpaper.

2 Using a large brush, apply the solution to the paper, working from the top down. Don't soak more than a few square yards at a time or the paper will dry out before you can strip it.

3 Let the paper soak for a few minutes, then strip it off with a scraper. It's a good idea to clean up each area as you work or the stripped wallpaper may dry out on your drop cloths and become hard to remove.

STRIPPING VINYL WALLPAPER

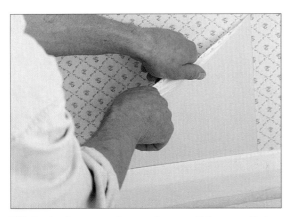

With vinyl papers, it may be possible to pull the top layer away from the backing paper without having to use a perforator. Don't be tempted to leave the backing paper on the wall, however, even if it's in good condition. It's not a good surface for painting.

IDEAL TOOLS

Spiker

Orbital scorer

With all types of wallpaper, it's a good idea to break the surface before soaking with stripper solution or hot water. There are several kinds of perforators, spikers, and scorers available, but all work in much the same way: They break through the top layer of paper, letting water and stripper underneath for easier, faster removal.

Priming and sealing

Priming is the first stage of painting a bare surface, whether it's wood, metal, or plaster. (Plaster surfaces are covered under Sealing; see pages 36–37.) Primer provides a surface to which the subsequent coats of paint bond, ensuring even coverage. With wood especially, primer prevents subsequent coats of paint from soaking into the surface. Just remember to choose the appropriate primer for each of the surfaces you're sealing.

Before painting new or bare wood, a shellac solution or sealer should be applied to all bare knots. This essential step will prevent sap from bleeding through and discoloring the paint that you apply later.

TOOLS: 1½-inch paintbrush, scraper, hot-air gun, small brush for sealer

MATERIALS: Steel wool, metal primer, sandpaper, solvent, clean cloth, sealer, wood primer

PRIMING METAL

1 Lightly rub copper pipes with a pad of fine steel wool. This will clean off any grime and provide tooth for the subsequent paint. Do this even if the pipes will stay unpainted—you'll find that it gives them an attractive polished finish.

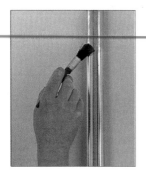

2 Although it's not essential to prime copper pipes, a coat of metal primer on any pipes that become heated, such as from a radiator, will help to prevent the top coat of paint from discoloring.

3 The most common ferrous-metal object in some homes is a radiator. Because it's a surface that gets hot, it must be painted when cold and primed with an oil-based metal primer. First sand the corroded areas back to shiny metal. Wipe off any dust with a clean cloth, then prime before oxidization occurs.

SEALING AND PRIMING PREVIOUSLY PAINTED WOOD

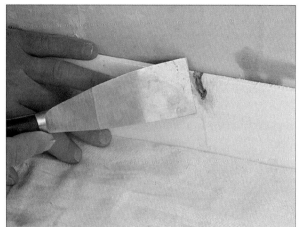

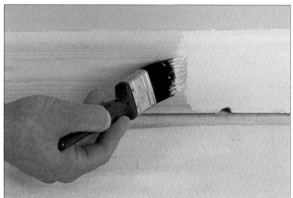

1 When treating a bleeding knot that has discolored the paint, remove the excess resin with a scraper. If the knot appears to be active, carefully heat it with a hot-air gun, letting all the resin bubble out. Continue to scrape the area clean until no more bleeding occurs. When using a hot-air gun, always read the manufacturer's instructions and follow the precautions on pages 32–33.

2 When the knot is completely free of resin, smooth the area of wood around it with sandpaper wrapped around a sanding block. When the wood is perfectly smooth, take a clean cloth, moisten it with solvent, and wipe off the area. This helps to pick up any remaining sanding dust or dirt and cleans the prepared surface so that it is ready for painting.

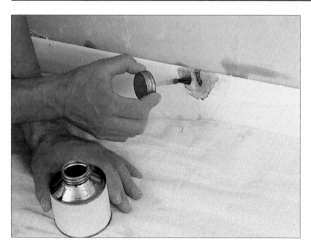

PRIMING BARE WOOD

3 Apply the sealer sparingly, slightly overlapping it onto the surrounding wood. Two coats usually are required for a good seal. Always allow the first to dry thoroughly before applying the second. Then patch-prime the knot area.

Work the primer along and into the grain of the wood. Because the primer is quite thin, apply it sparingly, otherwise runs may occur. On bare wood, make sure every area is covered. On previously painted wood, only bare spots need priming.

Patch ceilings and walls

Unfortunately, cracks and holes in plaster walls and ceilings are all too common. They're caused either by slight movement or settling in the structure or just everyday wear and tear. To repair them, use a commercially available filler or patching compound. Flexible fillers are best for areas of potential movement, such as the cracks around door trim. Premixed fillers come in plastic tubs ready to use, but powdered fillers that you mix with water let you prepare just the amount you need.

TOOLS: Dusting brush, putty knife, 1-inch paintbrush, broad knife, sanding block, hammer

MATERIALS: Powdered filler, water, fine-grit sandpaper, newspaper, batten, nails

1 Use the edge of a clean putty knife or scraper to rake out and clean up the damaged area. Brush out any loose debris with a dusting brush.

2 Pour the amount of powdered filler you need onto a clean surface. A lid from a plastic tub is ideal for this purpose. When estimating how much you should mix up at a time, remember that the filler will remain workable for about an hour. Gradually add water, mixing the filler into a creamy but firm consistency.

3 Dampen the hole and the area around it with water. This lengthens the drying time so the filler is less likely to shrink. It also helps the filler and the plaster to bond.

IDEAL TOOL

When patching an old wall with many small cracks, a broad knife will let you cover a large surface more quickly. Use it in the same manner as a putty knife. It's also excellent for wide holes where its large blade can rest on the edges of the hole, keeping the filler level.

4 Load some filler onto the putty knife and draw it across the hole, using the flexibility of the knife to firmly press the filler into the hole. You may need to draw the putty knife across the hole two or three times to make sure the area has been covered completely and that the filler is firmly in place. Always fill the hole slightly higher than the surrounding area to allow for a small amount of shrinkage. When the hole is filled, use the putty knife to clean off any excess filler from the wall around the hole to avoid any extra sanding when the filler dries.

5 When it's dry, sand the area with fine-grit sandpaper. Then run your fingers over the hole to make sure it's perfectly smooth and flush with the rest of the wall. If it's not, dust it off, wet it as before, and use a thin skim of filler to fill any indentations. Trying to fill particularly deep holes with filler in just one pass can be frustrating because bulging will occur where the filler is unable to bond with the surrounding area. In this case, it's best to use several thin coats to gradually build up the filler until it's level with the surrounding wall.

FILLING DEEP CRACKS

Sometimes it's necessary to fill a large, deep crack, such as in the corner of a room. Before filling it, wad up a piece of newspaper and, with a putty knife, press it firmly into the crack. This will give the filler a base on which to sit while it dries.

FILLING A CORNER

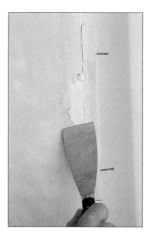

To repair an outside corner, attach a length of wooden batten flush to one edge of the corner, securing it with two nails. Fill the hole using a putty knife or a broad knife. When the filler is dry, sand the area, remove the batten, and repeat the process on the adjacent corner edge. Finally, fill the four nail holes you made when you tacked on the batten. This technique will restore the original square corner edge.

Stripping wood

When you're going to repaint wood, it's sometimes necessary to strip off all previous coats of paint—because the paint buildup is making your doors and windows stick or simply because fine details in the wood have become obscured by too many coats. Before you apply any natural wood finish, you *must* completely remove all traces of previous paint or varnish.

Basically, there are two ways to strip woodwork: by applying chemicals or by using a hot-air gun.

Ideally, doors should be taken off their hinges and laid flat on a workbench or on sawhorses. Always wear protective gloves and goggles, and protect the surrounding area with plenty of drop cloths.

TOOLS: Gloves, goggles, old paintbrush, scraper, shavehook, hot-air gun, putty knife, sanding block, electric sander, stiff brush

MATERIALS: Chemical stripper, white vinegar, clean cloth, stainable filler, sandpaper, solvent, steel wool

CHEMICAL STRIPPING

1 Although some chemical strippers are mixed into a paste and applied with a scraper or spatula, the most common are painted on. Use an old paintbrush to dab the stripper lightly on the painted surface, working in areas of approximately ½ square yard. Allow the stripper to react with the paint for 5 to 20 minutes, depending on the manufacturer's guidelines and the number of coats of paint to be removed.

2 Using a scraper or the flat edge of a shavehook, begin to remove the softened layers of paint. If all of the paint doesn't come off, you may need to let the chemicals react longer before trying to strip, or additional coats of stripper may be needed to remove especially thick layers of paint. Dispose of the stripper and paint scrapings in a sealed container or according to your community's waste-disposal guidelines.

PREPARING FOR A NATURAL WOOD FINISH

3 Dust off the sanded area using a brush or a clean cloth. When it's as dust-free as possible, wipe the entire surface using a clean cloth dampened with an appropriate solvent, and let it dry.

1 Cracks or defects on the stripped surface can be filled (see pages 34–35). For wood that will be finished with a natural wood treatment such as stain or varnish, always be sure to use a stainable filler.

2 As always, thorough sanding is essential for a smooth finish. For large surface areas, an electric sander saves both time and energy. When sanding, always work in the direction of the wood grain.

IDEAL TOOL

A shavehook is an ideal stripping tool. Its pointed corners are great for removing paint from the most intricate areas, such as the corners of door panels.

CLEANING

When all of the paint (or varnish) has been completely removed using a chemical stripper, the wood must be cleaned and the stripper chemicals neutralized so they won't continue to attack the wood or the new finish that you're about to apply.

The solution you use to clean the stripped area will depend on the solvent base of the stripper itself, so always read the manufacturer's instructions to determine which product to use. For example, one manufacturer simply recommends using ordinary white vinegar followed by scrubbing with a stiff brush and rinsing with clean water.

If any traces of paint remain stuck in the grain of the wood, dab a small amount of stripper on the area and rub gently with steel wool. Then, when the material has been removed, clean the area as before.

USING A HOT-AIR GUN

When using a hot-air gun, be careful not to point it at one area for too long—the heat will scorch the wood. Keep the gun moving slowly, only staying in one place long enough for the paint to begin to bubble. Then the paint is ready to be scraped off.

Filling wood

When preparing wood that you plan to paint, you can use the same types of filler that you use to repair holes in walls and ceilings. However, if the wood you're preparing will be stained or varnished, you'll want to use a stainable filler so you can color it to match and blend in with the surrounding wood.

    Powdered and premixed fillers are ideal for repairing chips in painted surfaces and for filling nail holes. However, for areas such as cracked door panels and door trim, flexible caulks and fillers that can ride out slight movement and normal settling are your best choice.

TOOLS: Hammer, nail set, putty knife, filler board, scraper, filler dispenser

MATERIALS: Sandpaper, powdered filler, flexible filler

POWDERED FILLER

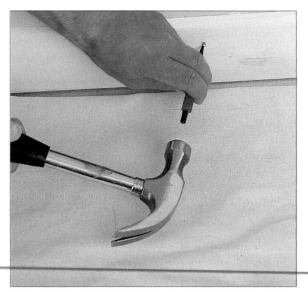

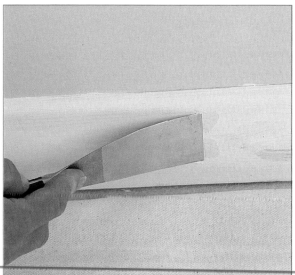

1 Before starting to fill an area such as a wooden baseboard, always check for popped nails. They'll spoil the final finish and may even cause an injury when the wood is sanded. Use a nail set and hammer to drive the nails back into and just below the surface of the wood.

2 Use a putty knife to fill the hole slightly higher than the surrounding area. Then wet the blade of the putty knife and draw it across the filled area, smoothing the filler to help reduce the amount of sanding needed. When the filler is dry, sand the wood smooth.

FLEXIBLE FILLER

1 When filling a cracked joint, rake out any loose paint or dust using the sharp edge of a scraper. Sand the area smooth and use a dusting brush to clear away the debris.

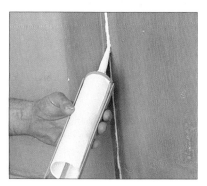

2 Cut the nozzle of the filler tube to the size you need. Gently pull the dispenser trigger while drawing the end of the nozzle down the crack, squeezing the filler into the gap.

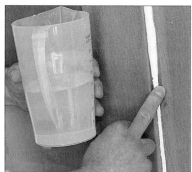

3 Run a wet finger over the filler, pushing it into the crack and creating a smooth finish. It's important to smooth the filler as soon as it's applied because it dries quickly.

3 For extensive bubbling and flaking on old painted surfaces, you may need to strip off all the paint and start with bare wood (see pages 32–33). However, in a small area, simply shave off the loose material using a scraper, being careful not to gouge the wood.

4 Sand down the area using medium-grit sandpaper on a sanding block. Then use fine-grit paper to feather the edges of the bare wood with the surrounding painted area. If the indentation still shows, skim on a thin layer of filler and sand smooth when it's dry.

Cleaning and sealing

Although they're not especially difficult, both of these steps are absolutely essential in preparing wall surfaces for any kind of decorating—whether it's new paint or wallpaper. So whatever you do, don't skip them.

These all-important steps won't show when your work is finished, but they'll go a long way toward making sure that you end up with a paint finish that's both good-looking and long-lasting.

TOOLS: Bucket, stirring stick, gloves, sponge, 1½-, 4-, and 5-inch paintbrushes

MATERIALS: Primer/sealer, water-based paint, moisture sealant or oil-based undercoat, aerosol stain block, all-purpose cleaner, water

CLEANING

1 Ceilings, walls, and woodwork should be cleaned using a solution of all-purpose cleaner or mild detergent. Mix it with warm water according to the manufacturer's instructions.

2 Wear protective gloves when using any cleaners that may irritate the skin. Make sure you clean all surfaces thoroughly, and that you remove any dust, debris, and impurities.

3 Rinse off all traces of the all-purpose cleaning solution using plenty of clean water and a sponge. When the area is completely clean, let the surface dry before continuing.

SEALING

1 Once your surfaces have been prepared and cleaned, seal all porous or dusty surfaces. Primers also can be used for this purpose, but on large areas they'll take longer to apply and tend to be less economical. A coat of primer/sealer solution provides both a sound surface for painting and acts as a "size" if you're preparing to hang lining paper. Always thoroughly read the manufacturer's guidelines and instructions for mixing the primer/sealer solution. The amounts and concentrations vary.

2 Apply the primer/sealer solution liberally for good coverage. Pick up any drips with your brush and work them back in. When it's dry, run your hand over the surface to make sure it's no longer dusty or powdery. If it is, apply a second coat.

3 New plaster surfaces can be primed or sealed in any number of ways, but water-based products are by far your easiest option. If you're going to paint directly on the plaster, diluted white water-based paint is ideal for two reasons. First, because the paint is permeable, any remaining moisture in the plaster can dry through the dried coat of paint. Second, it will give you a more uniform wall color and might even save you from having to apply more coats of paint than are necessary. Apply it evenly for best coverage (see pages 70–71).

COVERING MOISTURE STAINS

Moisture stains are common but will respond to the right treatment. Consult a professional if a damp patch is clearly active, because you may have an exterior water problem that needs attention. If the stain is old and dry or the problem has been corrected, apply a commercial sealant or an oil-based undercoat to the area.

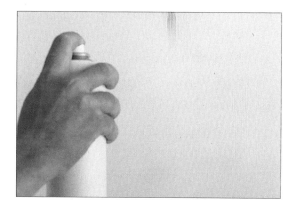

Some stains may continue to show through your paint finish. Commercial aerosol stain blocks usually will take care of marks like these that are the most difficult to cover.

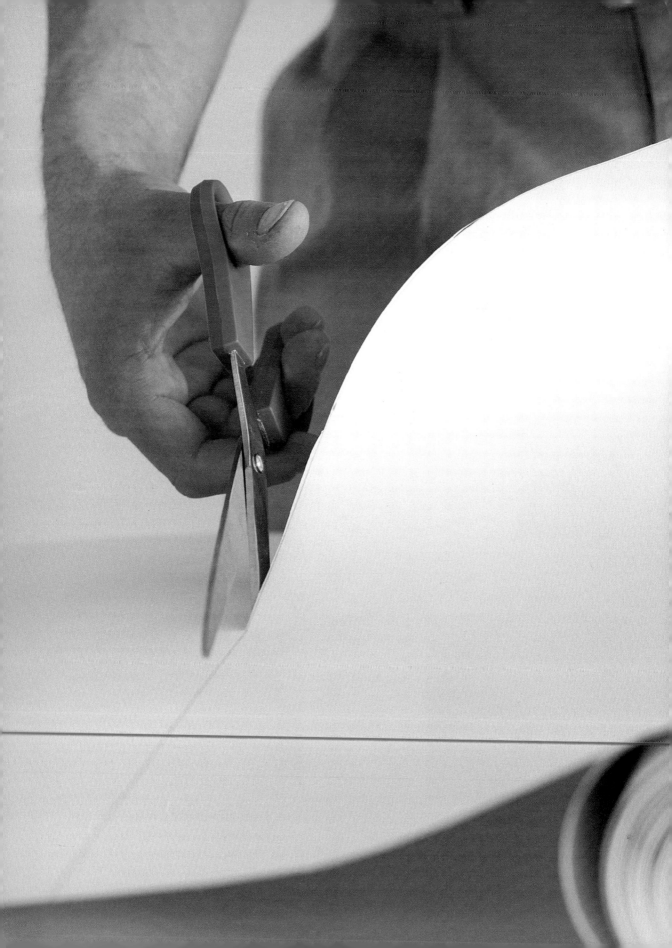

Lining

Whether you're planning to paint or paper a room, using lining paper on walls and ceilings makes the difference between a professional and an amateur finish. Lining paper smooths over imperfections and gives you an ideal surface on which to work. No wonder it's one of the best-kept secrets of professional painters and decorators.

You may have heard that you should hang lining paper horizontally for wallpapering and vertically for painting. Actually, it all comes down to practicality. You simply want to cover the walls and ceiling with the fewest number of lengths.

This chapter will show you the right way to hang lining paper and how to handle any problems you may encounter.

This chapter contains

Preparation

Before starting to hang any lining paper, decide how many rolls you need to complete the job. Using a tape measure and the table opposite, you can be amazingly accurate.

The diagram opposite shows the best way to calculate surface areas. There's no right or wrong place to start—just treat each surface separately. Mentally divide your room into different areas (see the illustration opposite) and determine the most practical direction in which to line; this also will help you plan your order of work. Begin with the ceiling; it's easier than most walls because there are fewer obstacles to work around.

When lining a wall horizontally, start at the top and work down; working from the bottom up causes problems when joining paper at high levels, especially after papering around an obstruction such as a doorway, window, or fireplace.

TOOLS: Tape measure, pocket calculator, bucket, liquid measuring cup, stirring stick

MATERIALS: Lining paper, wallpaper paste, water

1 When setting up your equipment, it's important to stay organized. Put the buckets of paste and clean water under the table to save space and to avoid accidents. Always keep your table clean and free of clutter. Try to keep everything handy to save time and energy.

2 When mixing up paste, make sure all equipment is clean. Always read the manufacturer's instructions; they vary from brand to brand. Measure out the correct amount of cold water using a liquid measuring cup.

3 Start to stir the water, then sprinkle the powder slowly into the bucket. Continue to stir for 2 minutes after adding all of the paste. Let it stand for another 3 minutes, then stir again to make sure there are no lumps. It's now ready to use.

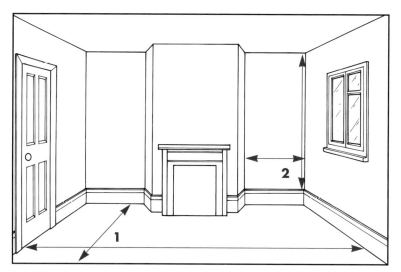

MEASURING

1 Measure these two lengths and multiply them to calculate the area of the ceiling.

2 Measure these two lengths and multiply them to calculate the area of the wall to the right of the fireplace. Use the same technique to work out the area of the other walls.

Don't deduct anything for doors and windows. You'll need to compensate for waste when you get to the trimming stage of applying the paper.

ROLLS OF LINING PAPER NEEDED

Total Surface Area to Line sq. yd.	No. of Rolls
6	1
12	2
18	3

For every additional 6 sq. yd., add 1 roll of lining paper.

A standard roll of lining paper is 22 inches×11 yards = $6\frac{3}{4}$ square yards. The excess of $\frac{3}{4}$ square yard per roll allows for both trimming and waste.

If you're not using standard rolls, don't worry. In that case, simply work out the surface area of the rolls you *are* using and create your own table just like the one above.

ORDER OF WORK

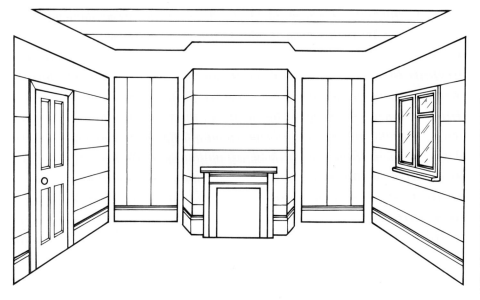

DOUBLE LINING

On especially uneven wall surfaces, the final finish may look better if you apply two layers of lining paper before painting. Make sure the seams on the second layer don't coincide with those on the first.

Cutting and pasting

When cutting lengths of lining paper, always add 4 inches to your base measurement to allow a 2-inch overlap at each end for final trimming.

After pasting, allow about 5 minutes for the paste to soak into the paper. This makes it less likely to bubble, more pliable, and easier to work with. Once you start work, it's a good idea to write a number on each length: You may have three or four lengths soaking at a time, and the numbers will keep them in the right order.

TOOLS: Pasting table, tape measure, pencil, steel rule, scissors, pasting brush, paper-hanging brush, sponge

MATERIALS: Lining paper, bucket of wallpaper paste, water

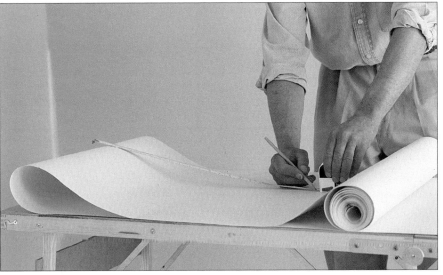

1 Carefully unroll the lining paper along the length of the pasting table. If long pieces of paper are going to be needed, gently fold the paper back on itself along the table. Use a tape measure to work out the length of paper needed. Make a pencil mark in the center of the paper where the first piece will be cut.

2 Keep the edges of the length of paper flush with the edges of the table. This will help you make a square cut. Place a straightedge at the pencil mark, check that it's square, and draw a line along it.

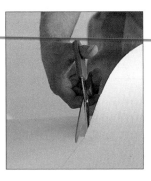

3 Cut a straight line along the pencil mark. Lay the paper flat along the table with the excess paper falling over one end. Use the paper-hanging brush to hold the other end.

4 Line up the paper flush with the edges of the table to avoid getting paste on the face of the paper. Apply the paste evenly, working from the center out and covering the whole area.

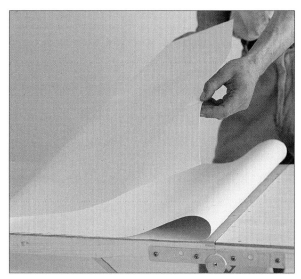

5 Once the paper on the table is pasted, gently fold the pasted end over. Pull it to one end of the table, again using the paper-hanging brush to anchor the other end.

6 Continue to paste the remaining paper, working up to the end of the table. Always make sure to apply the paste evenly, and to cover all areas of the paper with paste. And by all means, try to avoid getting any paste on the other (unpasted) side of the paper.

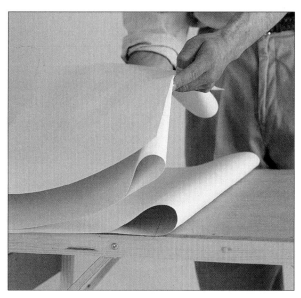

7 Keep folding the paper back on itself to make a nice, neat folded bundle that will be easy to lift. When all of the paper has been pasted, remove it from the table and let it soak for the required time. Wipe the table with a damp sponge to clean up any excess paste.

Ceilings

Always try to line across the longest dimension of the room because fewer lengths will be needed and this will save you lots of time. Make sure you have a solid platform to work on. Sawhorses and boards are perfect because they let you get close to the wall-ceiling junction at both ends of the platform. Adjust the height so the top of your head is about 9 to 12 inches from the ceiling.

Lining the ceiling isn't as difficult as it might appear. Once you hang the first length and establish a straight edge, the other lengths are easy.

TOOLS: Sawhorses and boards, paper-hanging brush, pencil, scissors, small brush for pasting edges, sponge

MATERIALS: Lining paper, bucket of wallpaper paste, water, clean cloth

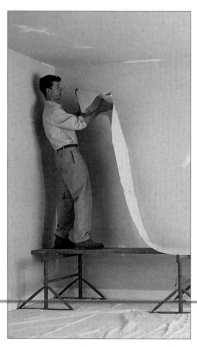

1 Arrange the sawhorses and boards under the area where you'll start. Carefully lay out the folded bundle of paper along the platform, and pick up one end.

2 Start papering at the edge of the ceiling. Be sure to keep the paper edge parallel to the adjacent wall. Using the paper-hanging brush, push the paper into the junction, allowing for about a 2-inch overlap.

3 When the paper is secure at one end, move slowly along the work platform, brushing the paper from the center out in a herringbone fashion. Keep the edge of the paper against the wall, using it as a guide. Brush it in place and repeat Step 2 at the other end.

4 When the length is hung, run a pencil along the line where the wall and ceiling meet. Or, simply run a pair of scissors along the line to make a crease.

EASIER CEILINGS
Papering a ceiling is easier and less tiring with two people. One holds the paper while the other puts it into its final, right position.

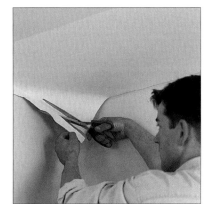

5 Carefully peel back the paper. Using paper-hanging scissors, cut a straight line along the pencil guideline or the scissors crease.

6 Push the paper back into position. Work along the length, checking for bubbles or lifting at the edges. Apply extra paste to edges where it's needed.

7 After each length is hung, immediately wipe off any excess paste from all surfaces to avoid staining.

Hang the next length in the same way, but place the edge of this new length adjacent to that of the first. Slide the paper into position to make a neat, tight, seamless butt joint.

Walk down the work platform, brushing out the paper and making sure the two edges of the joint remain tight. Trim off paper at each end as before.

DEALING WITH GAPS

If the wall isn't square, you'll find that a gap appears along the wall-ceiling junction as you work along the length of the ceiling. A small gap is relatively easy to fill (see page 51), but if a large gap appears, simply move the paper closer to the wall, allowing for an overlap onto the wall. Trim this overlap using the technique shown in Steps 4–6 above.

Ceiling fixtures

Most ceilings have at least one light fixture that you'll have to paper around. Two methods seem to work well. The first one is shown in Steps 1–5, and that is to pull the fixture cord through a cut in the paper. The second and more reliable method is shown in the box on page 47. For that technique, you'll measure the distance between the starting wall and the ceiling fixture to make sure that a seam falls at the point where the wiring leaves the ceiling.

TOOLS: Sawhorses and boards, paper-hanging brush, scissors, crafts knife, small paste brush, sponge, screwdriver

MATERIALS: Lining paper, bucket of wallpaper paste, water, clean cloth

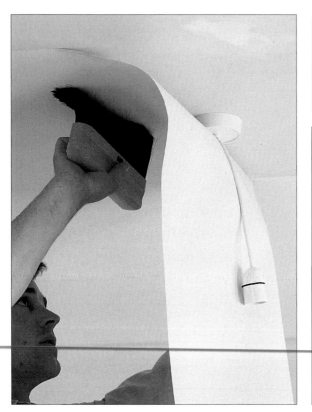

1 When you reach the ceiling fixture with a length of pasted paper, gently brush the paper over the fixture so that you can see its location on the paper.

ELECTRICAL SAFETY
Always remember to turn off the power before you start any wallpapering around electrical fixtures.

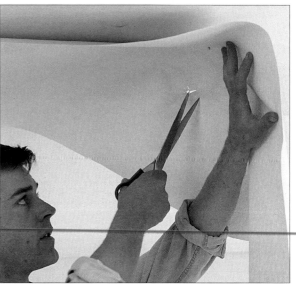

2 Support the unattached side of the paper with one hand. Using scissors, carefully mark the location of the center of the fixture on the underside of the paper. Make a small cut.

3 Gently pull the cord through the cut, being careful not to tear the paper. Then brush out the remaining length of paper, continuing on to the wall on the other side of the room.

4 Using scissors, make a series of small cuts out to the edges of the ceiling fixture. Work around the fixture, but don't cut any farther than the edges of the circular fixture itself.

5 Crease around the edges of the fixture and trim the paper with a crafts knife. Brush out any bubbles, and wipe off any excess paste found on the fixture's cord with a dry cloth.

METHOD 2: SEAM JOINT

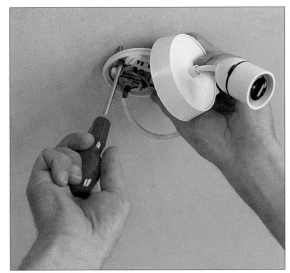

1 Turn off the power. Remove the fixture's cover, then loosen the retaining screws. Allow the entire wiring harness to drop about 2 inches.

2 Using the paper-hanging brush, tuck in the paper edges under the fixture base. Tighten the screws and reattach the ceiling-fixture casing.

Walls

You can hang lining paper on walls either horizontally or vertically. The choice is purely a practical one. Vertical lining is ideal for small alcoves because fewer lengths are required, but you can cover a long wall quickly with horizontal lengths. Vertical lining uses a vertical corner of the wall as a straightedge, and horizontal lining takes its guide from where the wall and the ceiling meet.

Because horizontal lengths usually are longer than vertical lengths, you'll have a larger folded wallpaper bundle. Use smaller folds to make the bundle more compact and easier to handle.

TOOLS: Sawhorses and boards, paper-hanging brush, pencil, scissors, crafts knife, small brush for pasting edges, sponge

MATERIALS: Lining paper, bucket of wallpaper paste, water

HORIZONTAL LINING

1 Start papering at the top of the wall, leaving a 2-inch overlap around the corner onto the next area of wall. Line up the top edge of the paper with the wall and ceiling junction. If the wall-ceiling junction isn't square, move the paper to overlap onto the ceiling and trim as usual when the rest of the length is hung.

2 Slowly release the folds of the bundle, smoothing the paper along the wall using a paper-hanging brush. Brushing from the center of the paper out, continue to the other corner, keeping the top edge of the paper flush with the wall-ceiling junction and following all of the previous tips.

3 Mark a line at the corner with a pencil, or crease the corner with scissors, then gently pull the paper away from the wall. Trim with the scissors or a crafts knife.

4 Push the paper back into the corner with the brush. Extra paste may be needed if the edge of the paper has dried out during trimming. Repeat Steps 3 and 4 at the other end of the length.

CROOKED ROOMS

If the wall or ceiling is very crooked (and you've had to overlap the paper onto the ceiling), you'll be unable to use the wall-ceiling junction as a guideline to hang the entire length. So you won't find yourself in the unenviable position of hanging this first length at an angle, hold a level at the bottom edge to ensure that the first length is hung straight. When lining vertically, a level also can be used as a guideline when out-of-square walls are causing the problem.

VERTICAL LINING

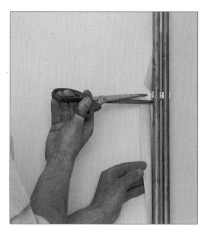

1 Vertical lining is an excellent way to deal with problems such as exposed pipes. Start the first length flush with the pipes and push the paper behind them so the seam will be hidden.

2 Mark the location of the pipe brackets with a pencil, and make two small cuts to the edges of the brackets. Push the paper around the brackets and trim off any excess.

3 Cut another length and butt-join it to the first length. Smooth and trim as before. Wipe any excess paste off the pipes, because it can react with any paint you might later apply.

Corners

When lining, the only corners you need to paper around are outside corners (that is, those that protrude). At inside corners, it's best simply to begin or end the wallpaper. Trying to bend it around the corner usually causes bubbles and problems with adhesion. Using sealant or filler on inside corners, as shown here, is a neater option. If you have difficulty with an outside corner that's uneven or out of square, an overlapping butt joint is the ideal solution.

TOOLS: Sawhorses and boards, paper-hanging brush, scissors, steel rule, crafts knife, sponge

MATERIALS: Lining paper, bucket of wallpaper paste, water, flexible filler, powdered filler, sandpaper, clean cloth

OUTSIDE CORNERS

1 Approach the outside corner holding the folded wallpaper bundle in one hand. Use the other hand to push the paper up to the corner edge, keeping the horizontal edge of the length of paper flush with the edge of the ceiling or the paper above. Form a neat butt joint.

2 Fold the paper around the corner using the paper-hanging brush to force out any air bubbles. Make sure the top edge of the paper isn't overlapping the paper already hung above it.

3 Run your fingers gently down the corner to check for any wrinkles or creases. Smooth them out, if necessary. Once the corner is neat and clean, proceed along the wall to position and secure the rest of the length.

UNEVEN OUTSIDE CORNERS

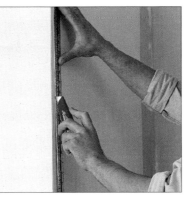

1 For an uneven corner, bend the horizontal length around the corner and trim off all except a 2-inch overlap. Do this with each (horizontal) length on the corner. Hang the next length (on the next section of wall) vertically, on top of the overlaps.

2 On the wall with the vertical length, place a straightedge 1¼ inches from the corner. Using a crafts knife, cut a straight line down the straightedge. Then move the straightedge and repeat the process, continuing the cut from ceiling to baseboard.

3 Pull back the paper and gently remove the excess (overlapping) strips of paper. Push the paper back into position using the paper-hanging brush. Finally, wipe the area with a damp sponge to remove any excess paste.

INSIDE CORNERS

1 Because we recommend trimming all lengths at an inside corner, for a perfect finish, run a bead of flexible caulk or filler along all inside corners and along the top of the baseboard.

2 Smooth along the filler with a wet finger. This will make a neater joint and prevent the edges of the paper from lifting later. Wipe off any excess filler with a clean, damp cloth.

FILLING GAPS

Small gaps between lengths sometimes are unavoidable. Fill them with commercial patching compound, then sand smooth.

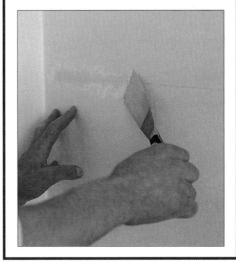

Doors and obstructions

Some room features—such as door trim, windows, and fireplaces—protrude from the wall, and that means you're going to have to cut lining paper to fit around them. No matter what the obstruction, the technique is the same. You'll get neat, clean results by carefully trimming into all of the angles and edges. The examples shown here include a fireplace that needs intricate trimming and a door.

TOOLS: Sawhorses and boards, paper-hanging brush, pencil, scissors, crafts knife, small brush for pasting edges, sponge

MATERIALS: Lining paper, bucket of wallpaper paste, water

FIREPLACES

2 After making this initial cut, ignore the paper fold on top of the fireplace for now. With your paper-hanging brush and your scissors, push the paper gently into the angles of the mantelpiece, making small right-angle cuts to let it lie flat against the wall.

3 Trim the small flaps with a crafts knife, being careful to get as close as possible to the molding and not to leave any gaps. Continue to paper along the top of the mantelpiece and repeat Steps 1–3 at the other corner. Then trim the fold on top of the mantelpiece.

1 When the paper reaches the fireplace, let it overlap the top corner of the mantelpiece. Make a cut diagonally toward the upper part of the corner, being especially careful that the paper below the cut doesn't tear under its own weight.

4 Always clean excess paste off ornate woodwork immediately in order to prevent staining or discoloring. Use a clean damp sponge, and pay special attention to paste that may have found its way into intricate cracks and details.

DOORS

1 Allow the length of paper to fall over the corner of the door trim. Continue to hang the length along the rest of the wall, loosely attaching it to the wall surface.

2 With both hands now freed, feel for the corner of the door trim. Cut diagonally toward this point with scissors. Carefully peel back the excess paper that hangs over the door. Using the paper-hanging brush, firmly push the paper covering the wall above the door into the edge of the door trim. Do the same at the other corner of the door trim.

3 Using a crafts knife, trim away all of the excess wallpaper, working very carefully around the side and top edges of the door trim.

Recessed windows

The technique for lining around a recessed window combines a number of steps already covered in this chapter. Still, the order in which you hang the lengths of paper is critical to getting the best results. As a bonus, the technique you learn here also will come in handy when you have to tackle similar types of shapes and obstructions, such as recessed doors and alcoves.

TOOLS: Sawhorses and boards, paper-hanging brush, scissors, crafts knife, small paste brush, steel rule, sponge

MATERIALS: Lining paper, wallpaper paste, water

1 Hang the first length of wallpaper horizontally as usual, letting it extend all the way across the recess. When you have the paper neatly butted against the previous length, return to the window and make two vertical cuts approximately ⅝ inch in from the corners of the recess. When you've done that, carefully continue these cuts all the way up to the top edge of the window recess to finish.

2 Starting in the middle, use the paper-hanging brush to push the flap of paper you've made back into the recess, brushing out any air bubbles as you go. Move the brush along the edge and continue the process until the paper is in place on the ceiling of the recess.

3 Make sure the paper is secure in the junction between the window frame and the upper part of the recess before trimming as usual.

4 Fold the ⅝-inch flap around the corner of the vertical recess, using your brush and fingers to expel any air bubbles if necessary. Add extra paste to the edge of the paper if it happens to have dried out too quickly. Hang the next length, again allowing a flap of paper approximately ⅝ inch wide to fold around into the recess. Then simply repeat this process at the opposite side of the window recess.

5 Depending on the height of the window recess, you may need to hang more lengths of paper before finally reaching the windowsill. At the sill, carefully trim the paper using a series of right-angle cuts, molding the paper around the corner of the sill and underneath it. When you've completed one side of the window, simply repeat this step when the paper reaches the opposite corner of the sill.

6 Measure and cut a panel of paper to line each vertical area of the recess. Line up the straight edge of the paper with the vertical corner, covering the trimmed overlaps of the previous paper lengths.

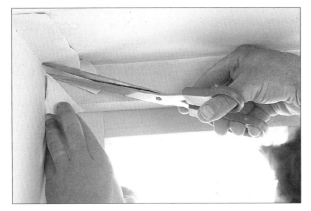

7 Make diagonal cuts into the top corner of the recess. Repeat at the bottom corner to help with the final trimming. Fill any small gaps as shown on page 51.

REFINING YOUR TECHNIQUE
You may find that this technique of overlapping different pieces of lining paper doesn't produce a completely flat surface: The small cuts around the vertical outside corners of the recess may show under the paper you paste over the top. When this happens, there are two points to consider. First, it's likely that curtains will eventually cover these imperfections. Second, as you become more skilled, you may prefer to make an overlapping butt joint as shown in Uneven Outside Corners (page 51).

Switches and outlets

It goes without saying that light switches and electrical outlets are common features on walls, but it may seem difficult to paper around them. Fortunately, if you take your time, they're no problem at all. It's especially important to do a neat job on light switches because every time you enter or leave a room, your eyes are naturally drawn toward them. Whatever their size or shape, the technique for papering around them is the same.

Always remember to turn off the power at the circuit breaker before working near any electrical switch or outlet.

TOOLS: Sawhorses and boards, paper-hanging brush, pencil, scissors, screwdriver, crafts knife, small brush for pasting edges, sponge

MATERIALS: Lining paper, bucket of wallpaper paste, water, dry cloth

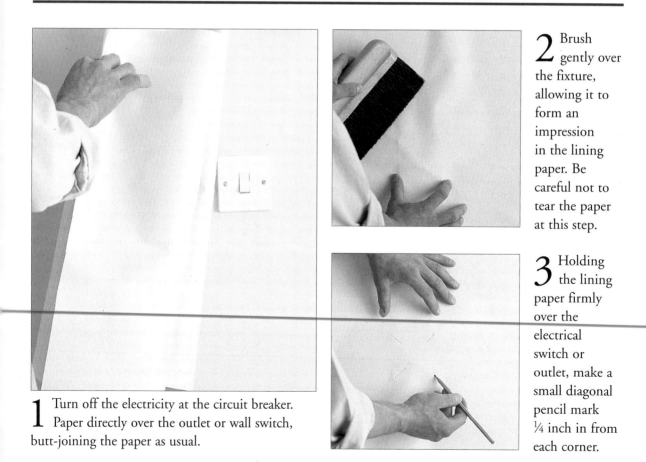

1 Turn off the electricity at the circuit breaker. Paper directly over the outlet or wall switch, butt-joining the paper as usual.

2 Brush gently over the fixture, allowing it to form an impression in the lining paper. Be careful not to tear the paper at this step.

3 Holding the lining paper firmly over the electrical switch or outlet, make a small diagonal pencil mark ¼ inch in from each corner.

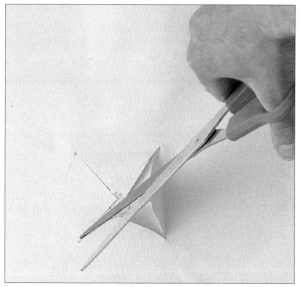

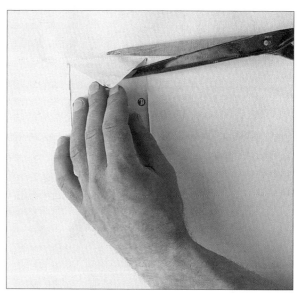

4 Using scissors, carefully make four diagonal cuts from the center of the switch out to the pencil marks.

5 Trim off each of the four flaps just inside the outer edges of the switch so a small overlap remains over the switch plate.

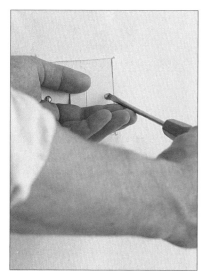

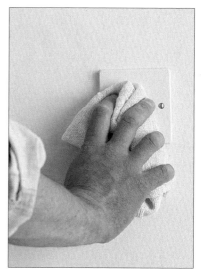

6 Unscrew the two retaining screws that hold the cover plate onto the switch. It's not necessary to unscrew them completely—just far enough to move the cover plate away from the wall.

7 Ease the cover plate away from the wall, rotating it slightly from side to side. Be careful when pushing the cover plate through the paper so you don't tear it. Use the brush to push the paper behind the plate.

8 Wipe off any excess paste with a dry cloth. Put the cover plate back and tighten the screws, making sure the small paper flaps are firmly tucked behind the plate. Be careful not to overtighten the screws.

Wall-mounted fixtures

It can be hard to paper around wall-mounted fixtures such as lights and central-heating radiators, so it's usually best to remove them. However, removing a radiator may be next to impossible if the plumbing is old and the joints are frozen. Wall fixtures usually are easy to take down, but if for some reason they're not, leave them in place and just be careful to keep paste off brass and other metal trim that it could stain or tarnish. Obviously, papering around electrical fixtures needs to take place during the day so you can see what you're doing when the power is off.

TOOLS: Screwdriver, scissors, pencil, paper-hanging brush, roller, small brush for pasting edges, sponge

MATERIALS: Electrical tape, lining paper, bucket of wallpaper paste, water

LIGHT FIXTURES

1 Remember to turn off the power at the circuit breaker before starting work. Unscrew the wall-mounted light fixture, being careful to support its weight as you do.

2 Using electrical tape, cover the exposed wires. Replace the fixture's screws in the wall. It may be useful to draw a diagram of the wiring layout to help when you replace the fixture later.

3 Paper over the area. Use a pencil to mark on the paper the location of the base of the wires. Pull the paper back and make a small cut where the wiring will go through. Then pull the wires through the paper.

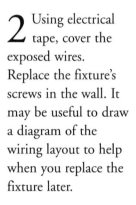

4 Using a paper-hanging brush, smooth the paper and let the wall screws break through its surface. Trim the paper as necessary. Do not replace the fixture until you're sure you've completed all of your painting.

RADIATORS

IDEAL TOOL

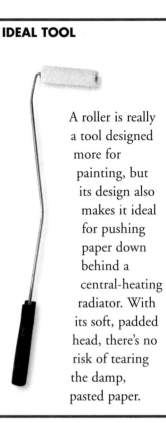

A roller is really a tool designed more for painting, but its design also makes it ideal for pushing paper down behind a central-heating radiator. With its soft, padded head, there's no risk of tearing the damp, pasted paper.

1 When you get to a radiator, place the paper over the top, keeping the butt joint flush. Then carefully pull the paper away from the wall to reveal the radiator's supporting brackets.

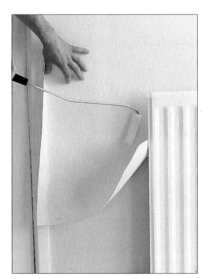

2 Holding the length of paper over the front of the radiator, mark the locations of the two supporting brackets with a pencil.

3 Using scissors, make a vertical cut from the bottom of the paper to the pencil marks. Do this for each supporting bracket.

4 Using the roller, push the paper into position on each side of the brackets, and wipe off any excess paste.

Cleaning up

When all of your painting is done, it's time to clean up. Granted, this isn't something to look forward to. But you don't want to find stiff brushes, grimy buckets, and paste-covered scissors when you start your next painting project. It's not only inconvenient but potentially expensive if you have to replace ruined equipment.

Store unused rolls of lining paper in a dry place, and tape any opened rolls to prevent them from unrolling and becoming damaged and unusable.

TOOLS: Sponge, bucket with lid, nail

MATERIALS: Detergent, clean cloth, water

1 Wash the paper-hanging brush under warm running water, using household detergent to remove any dry paste. Rinse thoroughly and allow to dry before storing. To clean the pasting brush, remove as much paste from the bristles as you can. Then wash, rinse, and dry in the same way.

2 Rinse the paper-hanging scissors under warm water, sponging off any dry paste that might dull the cutting edges. Be especially careful to thoroughly dry every part of the scissors with a clean cloth so you'll be able to prevent any possibility of corrosion.

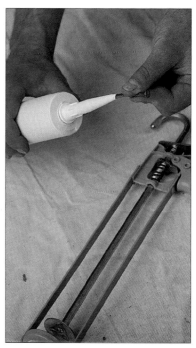

3 If you've overestimated and you have leftover paste but you're likely to need more in the near future, it can be safely and successfully stored for a few weeks in an airtight container.

4 Wipe the table with clean water and a sponge, paying special attention to the edges where paste usually collects. Fold up the table to store it only when it's completely dry.

5 It's important to seal a partly used tube of flexible caulk, sealer, or filler, so it doesn't dry out and become impossible to use again. To do this, just place a nail in the end of the nozzle.

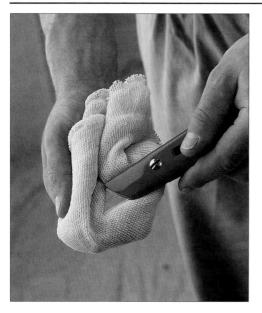

6 Before storing or putting away a crafts knife, it should be carefully wiped clean with a damp cloth to remove all traces of wallpaper paste. Then dry it thoroughly. For safety reasons, always dispose of old blades—even if they're dull—by placing them in a container, such as an empty paint can. Make sure the can is sealed securely before disposing of it in any way. Or better yet, recycle all of your used crafts-knife blades if that's an option in the community where you live.

PASTE DISPOSAL

Most wallpaper paste contains fungicide and isn't biodegradable. Wallpaper paste never should be poured down a drain because it could pollute the water supply. Instead, dispose of it according to your community's solid-waste guidelines.

Painting

With all the dirty work done—the sanding, filling, priming, and general preparation—the actual painting can be the most enjoyable part of redecorating your home. This chapter demonstrates all the different techniques and methods for applying both undercoats and finish coats to all interior surfaces. Always read the manufacturer's instructions for the number of coats recommended for each kind of paint, and follow our recommendations on Order of Work (see pages 14–15). Remember, don't skimp on drying time between coats and never rush your work—or you might spoil your results.

Preparation

The order in which you paint is important and goes a long way toward making sure you only have to paint a particular area once. There's nothing more frustrating than having to repaint something because of poor planning. As a rule of thumb, paint the ceiling first, followed by the walls, and then the woodwork. This order will make sure that splatters from the ceiling onto the walls and overlaps from the walls onto the woodwork will be covered by the next stage of painting. Designate smaller items, such as window trim, as finishing touches and save them for the end. Whether you're using solvent- or water-based paints, avoid breathing paint fumes, and open all available doors and windows to ensure adequate ventilation.

TOOLS: Dusting brush, lid opener, stirring stick, paint bucket, aluminum foil, gauze cloth, large rubber band, scraper

MATERIALS: Paint, masking tape

PREPARING THE PAINT

1 Before opening the paint can, use a dusting brush to wipe off the lid because grit and dirt tend to collect around the rim. If you don't do this, debris may fall into the paint as you remove the lid.

Pry the lid open with a blunt tool. A special lid opener is designed just for this purpose and will avoid wear and tear on your good screwdrivers and chisels.

2 Some paints, such as nondrip gloss and solid water-based paints, shouldn't be stirred before use, so always read the manufacturer's instructions. Otherwise, most paints need a thorough stirring. Use either a commercial stirring stick or a piece of wooden dowel. As you stir, use a lifting motion. This brings up any sediment from the bottom of the can and ensures that the pigments are mixed thoroughly.

3 There are several good reasons for decanting the paint into a plastic or metal paint bucket. First, the original paint can will stay cleaner for storage and it's next use. Second, if the paint bucket is knocked over or dropped, less paint will be spilled. And finally, if any debris gets into the bucket, it can be cleaned out and refilled from the original can. Lining your paint bucket with aluminum foil will save time when cleaning up or switching to a different color of paint.

4 When using paint left over from a previous job, you may find that a skin has formed over the paint's liquid surface. Remove it from the can before attempting to stir the paint. The paint may still have lumps, so it's a good idea to strain it before use. Place some stockinette material or gauze cloth over the paint bucket, and hold it in place with a large rubber band. Pour the paint slowly into the bucket; the lumps will be trapped on top of the cloth.

NONDRIP PAINTS

Solid water-based and other nondrip paints have been formulated to make painting easier. They don't need stirring and they make less mess during painting because of their special consistency.

MASKING

It's not always possible to take up the carpet in a room before painting. Protect it by applying masking tape to the edges and using a scraper to push it under the baseboard. The tape will keep carpet fibers off the painted baseboard as well as keep paint off the carpet when you paint the woodwork. Remove the tape before the final coat hardens completely, or you might damage the paint surface.

Using a roller

Using a roller is the quickest and most efficient way of covering large interior surfaces. Although you certainly can use rollers to apply solvent-based paints, you'll find they're usually used with water-based paints. Your choice of roller covers is now greater than ever, with a variety of sizes and textures that makes them practically indispensable for the do-it-yourself painter.

TOOLS: Rollers, roller tray, textured roller cover, extension handle, roller shield

MATERIALS: Paint, plastic wrap

1 A roller tray consists of two parts: the paint reservoir, and a ribbed slope to wipe off excess paint and allow it to run back into the reservoir. Pour the prepared paint into the tray's reservoir to just below the start of the slope.

2 Dip the roller into the paint reservoir and run it firmly up and down the ribs of the slope to distribute the paint evenly around the roller cover. Be careful not to overload the roller or you'll drip and spatter the paint.

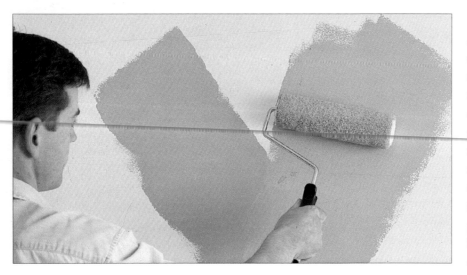

3 Move the loaded roller over the wall surface using light, even strokes. Don't move the roller too fast or you'll cause a fine mist of paint overspray. Each time the roller is reloaded, apply it to an unpainted surface and then work back to the previously painted area in a series of overlapping diagonal strokes.

SPECIAL ROLLERS AND TOOLS

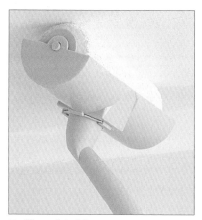

Extension handles

These attach to the roller handle and are especially handy for painting ceilings and stairwells. But don't save them just for heights: An extension handle also reduces the amount of bending you do when you reload the roller or paint areas low on the walls.

Textured rollers

Textured paints are similar to very thick water-based paints. They're excellent for covering up small cracks. Here, a textured roller cover is used to create a stippled effect. The paint tends to dry quickly, so you'll want to work on only a small area at a time—about 1 square yard.

Roller shield

A roller with a plastic shield is a useful tool whenever you have to paint a ceiling. It helps avoid both roller spray and drips from the edges of the roller frame. Some shields attach to extension handles for painting ceilings; check that the shield fits the handle you'll be using.

4 Work around and behind awkward areas such as pipes and radiators with a long-handled, low-profile roller designed just for this purpose. They make tight spots easier to paint.

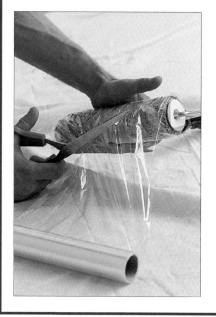

TEMPORARY STORAGE

When you have to stop temporarily during painting—between coats, for example—wrap a short length of plastic wrap around the roller head, being careful not to trap any air. This avoids having to repeatedly clean and dry the roller and roller cover.

Pads and sprayers

Paint pads, sprayers, and spray guns are alternatives to the more traditional rollers and brushes.

Paint pads create less spray and are less messy than rollers. Their design also has improved over the years, so that now they can be used successfully, not just for covering large flat surfaces, but also for small, intricate areas such as window and door trim.

Airless spray guns also have become more efficient and even have gone down in price, bringing them within reach of the do-it-yourself painter. The technique for spraying is surprisingly easy to master, and the professional results are nothing short of spectacular.

TOOLS: Paint pads, paint tray, paint sprayer, goggles, respirator mask, gloves, drop cloths

MATERIALS: Masking tape, paint

PAINT PADS

1 Paint pads are flat and rectangular with closely packed, short, fine fibers. When used carefully, they produce a smooth paint finish. Pads come in a variety of sizes for all-purpose use.

2 When loading a paint pad, gently dip the fibers into the tray reservoir. Be careful not to immerse the pad head; this will leave drips when you apply the pad to the wall. Pull the pad over the ribbed slope to distribute the paint. Some trays come with a built-in ribbed roller to remove the excess paint.

3 To paint the wall, make light, even strokes in all directions, slightly overlapping each stroke. Pads require reloading more often than rollers because they can't hold as much paint.

Paint pads tend to be faster than a brush but slower than a roller. Although pads apply paint very evenly, they tend to produce thinner coverage than brushes and rollers, so you may need to apply extra coats. Extension handles also fit paint-pad heads to reach awkward areas such as ceilings.

PAINT SPRAYERS

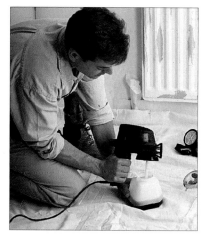

1 Mask all surrounding areas that you don't want to paint. Thin the paint if necessary, following the manufacturer's instructions, and pour it into the reservoir of the spray gun. Attach the reservoir to the gun, and choose the correct nozzle for the type of paint you have and the finish you want.

2 It's a good idea to test the spray gun and your spraying technique on some old newspaper before starting the actual project. The paint spray may spatter slightly when the gun is started, so aim the gun away from the area you want to paint, then slowly sweep it back when the spray is more uniform.

3 As you spray, use a steady, deliberate motion, slightly overlapping the paint that you've already applied. Never be tempted to return to a patchy area: The paint may run if you apply too much at once. Several thin coats are always better than just one or two thicker coats.

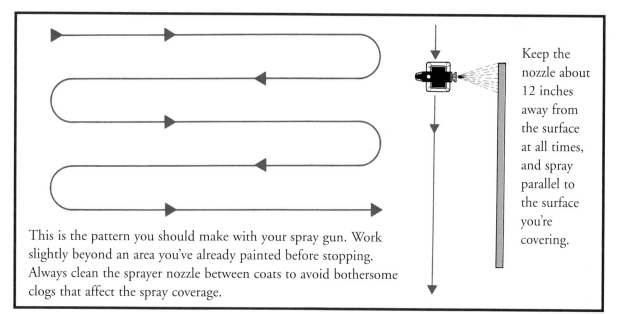

Keep the nozzle about 12 inches away from the surface at all times, and spray parallel to the surface you're covering.

This is the pattern you should make with your spray gun. Work slightly beyond an area you've already painted before stopping. Always clean the sprayer nozzle between coats to avoid bothersome clogs that affect the spray coverage.

Using a brush

Brushes have always been the most popular and versatile tools for painting just about any surface. There are brushes that can handle almost any problem—from painting large areas to getting into the seemingly unreachable gaps behind toilet tanks. Pure-bristle brushes are still the professional choice, but synthetic alternatives also are popular. Brush prices vary considerably, and it's worth paying a little extra for quality. Cheap brushes are stiff, have shorter bristles, and shed more bristles, making a good finish hard to achieve.

TOOLS: 4- to 5-inch paintbrush, paint bucket, vacuum cleaner, paint shield

MATERIALS: Paint, clean cloth, solvent

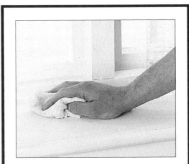

1 Before starting to paint, flick the end of the brush and wipe it on a lint-free cloth to remove any loose bristles and dust. If possible, use the new brush for priming or undercoating first to get rid of any loose bristles. Then, when the brush is broken in, use it to apply your finish coats of paint.

2 Dip the brush into the paint so that about one-third of the bristles are immersed. Raise the brush and gently push the bristles against the side of the paint bucket to remove excess paint. Avoid scraping the brush on the edge of the bucket; this will build up paint on the inside and cause drips down the outside.

FINAL CLEANING

Even after the most thorough preparation and cleaning of the surfaces you'll paint, dust still accumulates on horizontal areas such as windowsills. Just before painting, wipe them with a lint-free cloth dampened with a little solvent. They'll dry quickly when the solvent evaporates, leaving a completely dust-free surface for your professional paint finish.

3 When using water-based paint on a large area, such as a wall, choose a 4- to 5-inch paintbrush; a larger brush will be too heavy and will quickly tire your arm. Apply the paint to the wall with short, overlapping horizontal and vertical strokes of the brush, working in areas of approximately 1 square yard at a time.

4 With the brush unloaded, remove any visible brush marks by lightly drawing the bristles across the painted surface, again using a series of horizontal and vertical strokes. This technique is known as "laying off." When you're finished, move on to the adjoining area, always working away from the wet edge.

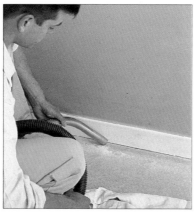

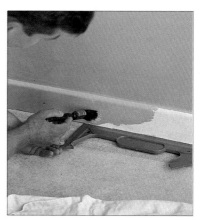

5 When applying solvent-based paint to a large area, make three vertical, parallel strips that are about 12 inches long. Without reloading the brush, blend the strips together horizontally, brushing out the paint. Finish by making several light vertical strokes.

6 Always keep the painting area as clean and dust-free as possible. A vacuum cleaner is the most efficient way of keeping the room clean, and it's especially handy at baseboard level. If any dirt or grit gets on the baseboards, sand them lightly between coats.

7 When painting a baseboard, place a paint shield or a clean piece of cardboard against the bottom, parallel to the floorboards or carpet. This will ensure you don't pick up dirt from the floor and move it to the painted surface. It also will protect your floor.

Cutting in

Although rollers and paint pads are efficient for covering large areas such as walls and ceilings, there are still plenty of corners and edges to be painted. This is what's known as "cutting in."

When using a roller, for example, you can cut in either before or after rolling the adjacent areas, as long as the paint edges are still wet. Wet and dry paint edges on the same coat give your wall an unattractive framed look. When drying conditions are quick, as is the case with most water-based paints, finish painting each wall or ceiling before moving on to the next area. That way, you'll have the best chance of keeping paint edges wet at all times.

TOOLS: 2- to 2½-inch paintbrush, fitch brush, corner roller, small paint pad

MATERIALS: Paint, clean cloth, solvent, masking tape

CORNERS

1 When cutting in up to a surface that's already painted, you're going to have to apply the paint especially carefully to get a truly professional finish. You'll find that a 2- to 2½-inch brush is an ideal size for this job. Load the brush with paint, and apply about a 20-inch strip slightly away from the corner.

2 With the brush now unloaded, spread the paint up to the corner junction, using the splayed edge of the bristles. Cut in right into the corner, creating a neat, straight line. For greater precision, you may need to repeat this process two or three times to move the paint exactly into the junction.

3 In the corner of the room or at a tight angle near built-in furniture, it's sometimes easiest to use a small, flat, angled fitch brush rather than a paintbrush, even if it's a small one. The finer angled bristles of the fitch brush make it easier to get into the corner for painting that's perfectly square and straight.

SWITCHES AND OUTLETS

1 When cutting in around small obstructions such as electrical outlets and light switches, a fitch brush may be more precise and easier to use than a larger brush.

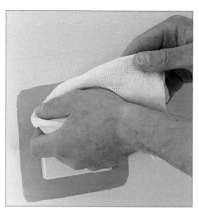

2 Be sure to remove any paint from the switch or outlet while it's still wet. Use a cloth slightly dampened with either water or solvent, depending on the type of paint you're using.

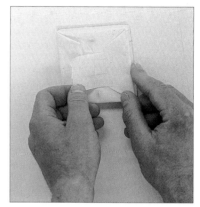

3 Although it's more time-consuming, you also can use masking tape to cover switches and outlets. This makes sense for intricate cover plates that are hard to clean.

4 Along an edge where both painted surfaces will be the same color, you can use a corner roller instead of cutting in with a paintbrush. Be careful not to overload the roller with paint or you'll almost certainly leave roller trails and end up with varying thicknesses of paint, detracting from the final finish.

5 Small paint pads give you an excellent edge when cutting in next to a surface of a different color. Line up the pad's top edge against the ceiling and draw it across the wall. Pads won't work if the corner is uneven, though; they're not very flexible and can't conform to out-of-square corners.

OVERLAPPING EDGES

In this example, notice how the ceiling paint was overlapped onto the wall. This is a timesaving tactic, because there's no reason to cut in at a corner or ceiling with *both* paint colors. The second color will always cover up the overlap when you cut it in.

Doors

Doors get more wear and tear than just about any other painted area in the home. Solvent-based paints have been the finish of choice for this job, just because they're so hard-wearing. But whatever paint you use, the trick is to apply it in a logical order.

Remove all door hardware before starting so you'll avoid having to cut in around it. This is also a good time to clean and repair it, if necessary.

TOOLS: 1-, 2-, and 3-inch paintbrushes, paint bucket

MATERIALS: Paint

FLUSH DOOR

1 Mentally divide the door into eight sections, and, starting in the top left-hand corner, work from left to right and down. Use a 2- to 3-inch brush for quick coverage and minimal brush marks. And always be especially careful not to overload the wet edges of each section; doing so may result in runs and sags.

2 As you cover each section of the door, make a series of light upward strokes with the brush to even out the paint. When you're through with this step, use a smaller brush to paint the edges of the door, as well as the door frame and the door trim. Use the diagram on page 75 as a guide for identifying the door components.

Color divisions on a door and doorway

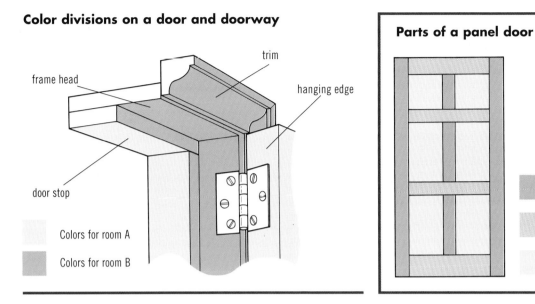

trim

frame head

hanging edge

door stop

Colors for room A

Colors for room B

Parts of a panel door

stiles

members

panels

PANEL DOOR

1 Using a 2-inch brush, begin with the top panels, doing the moldings first. Work your way down, painting all the panels in sequence. Paint runs often happen at panel corners, so be prepared to brush them out—possibly even more than once.

2 Again, starting from the top of the door, paint the center vertical stiles. Take care not to brush too far onto the horizontal members (the areas between the panels) because the vertical brush marks may show through the final coat.

3 When the center vertical stiles are painted, paint the three horizontal members. Always remember to even out the paint only in the natural direction of the grain of the wood.

4 Paint the outer vertical stiles. Then, using a smaller brush, paint the door edges. Try to avoid getting paint on the hinges. Last, paint the door frame and trim. Remember to prop the door open while it dries.

Casement windows

Windows are tricky to paint, but by working in a logical sequence, you can keep the frustration factor to a minimum and still achieve good results. Doing a thorough job on your windows is especially important when you consider that, of all the areas in the home, they're the most affected by weather. Direct sunlight, moisture and condensation, as well as expansion and contraction of joints, all take their toll.

Try to paint windows early in the day so they don't have to stay open all night to dry.

TOOLS: Screwdrivers, 1½-inch paintbrush, paint bucket, small angle-headed brush

MATERIALS: Paint, clean cloth, masking tape

Parts of a casement window

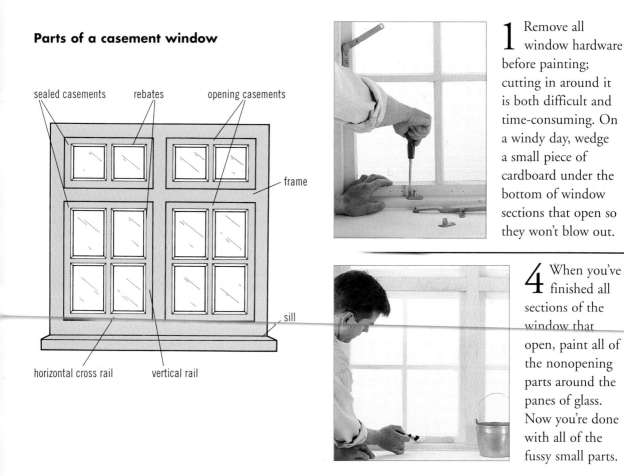

sealed casements   rebates   opening casements

frame

sill

horizontal cross rail   vertical rail

1 Remove all window hardware before painting; cutting in around it is both difficult and time-consuming. On a windy day, wedge a small piece of cardboard under the bottom of window sections that open so they won't blow out.

4 When you've finished all sections of the window that open, paint all of the nonopening parts around the panes of glass. Now you're done with all of the fussy small parts.

METAL WINDOWS

Painted metal windows are prepared and repainted in exactly the same way as their wooden counterparts. However, if they show any patches of rust, they should be cleaned thoroughly down to sound, bare metal and then treated with metal primer.

Aluminum and vinyl windows usually need very little maintenance, and in fact, probably weren't designed to be painted. To keep them clean and bright, simply wash them with a solution of warm soapy water. Never use abrasive cleaners on either aluminum or vinyl windows because they can scratch and abrade the surface.

MASKING WINDOWPANES
Although it's definitely time-consuming, masking individual panes is one way to keep paint off glass surfaces. This is an especially good option for the beginning painter who may not have completely mastered the technique of cutting in with a brush. If you mask the individual panes, remember to remove the tape while the top coat is still tacky; otherwise, you risk damaging the newly painted surface.

2 Mentally divide the window into smaller sections, and begin by painting all the parts that open. As usual, start out at the top of the window. Here, the small openable window is being painted first.

3 Paint the lower opening sections of the window. With each separate section, paint the window rebates first and then work out to the cross rails and vertical rails.

5 Finish by painting the larger parts: the outer window frame and the sill. Keep returning to the window to check for paint runs, which are especially common at the rebate-rail junctions.

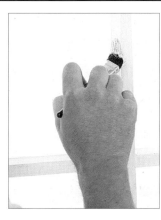

6 Painting window rebates requires a technique similar to cutting in (see page 72). Again, you'll need to cut in the paint right up to the wood-glass junction. This will be easier if you use a small angle-headed brush.

Sash windows

Due to their design, sash windows appear to be difficult to paint. But if you follow the correct sequence, they're just as easy as any other painting job.

If the paint on the runners is basically sound, leave these areas alone. Too many coats of paint can jam the window. It's also important to keep paint away from the sash cords so they run freely.

TOOLS: Fitch brush, 2-inch paintbrush, paint bucket, window guard, window scraper

MATERIALS: Paint, masking tape

Parts of a sash window

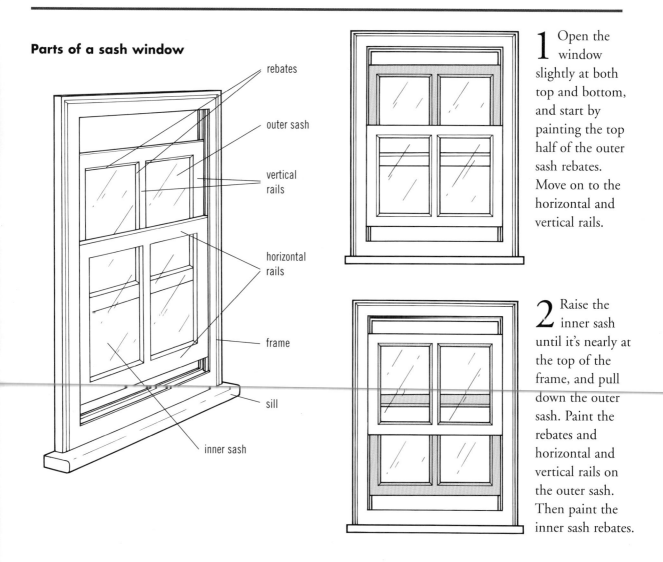

rebates

outer sash

vertical rails

horizontal rails

frame

sill

inner sash

1 Open the window slightly at both top and bottom, and start by painting the top half of the outer sash rebates. Move on to the horizontal and vertical rails.

2 Raise the inner sash until it's nearly at the top of the frame, and pull down the outer sash. Paint the rebates and horizontal and vertical rails on the outer sash. Then paint the inner sash rebates.

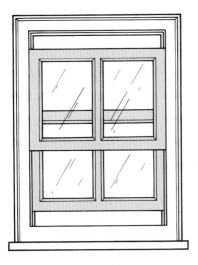

3 Leave the sashes in the same position as in Step 2, and finish painting the inner sash. Then paint the exposed lower runners, taking care not to touch or smudge the wet paint on the two sashes.

4 Return the window to its original position (see Step 1) and paint the upper runners. The top and bottom edges of the inner sash can now be painted. Finally, paint the surrounding frame and sill.

Parts of a sash window-mechanism

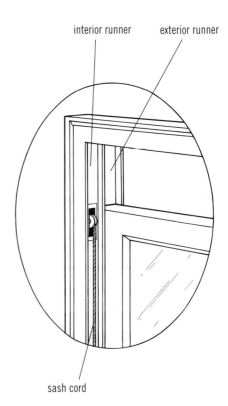

interior runner   exterior runner

sash cord

IDEAL TOOLS

Window guards

Saves time by keeping paint off the glass. Hold the guard tightly against the glass and the rebate, paint around the pane, and move the guard to the next area. Window guards are less effective on older windows, where uneven rebates and small joint variations let paint squeeze out under the guard's edges. Wipe off the guard often to avoid paint buildup and smudging.

Window scraper

Handy for removing excess paint or spray from the glass of the window after the paint has dried.

Fitch

Useful for painting the runners, where it's important to keep paint off the sash cords for smooth window operation.

Metal

Household hardware and trim can be made from a variety of metals. For example, radiators commonly are made from ferrous metals, which are prone to rust; copper pipes and aluminum are nonferrous and don't corrode as much. You'll find that the hardware on windows and doors may be made of either type of metal.

Remove as much of the hardware from your doors and windows as you can. This will make painting the doors and windows—and the hardware—much easier.

TOOLS: Fitch brush, 1½- and 2-inch paintbrushes, paint bucket, wire brush, scraper, screwdriver

MATERIALS: Heat-resistant, solvent-based, and aerosol paints; steel wool; clean cloth; lumber

HEATED METAL SURFACES

1 Always prepare and paint an object that gets hot only when it's cold. Otherwise, the paint will dry too quickly, producing an uneven, blotchy finish. On cast iron, such as on a wood-burning stove or a fireplace, use a wire brush to remove any loose material, then dust the area. Wipe it clean using a cloth dampened with the appropriate solvent to remove any remaining particles.

2 Because a cast-iron stove or fireplace may reach a very high temperature when it's being used, apply a paint specifically manufactured for heated cast-iron surfaces. Paints that aren't heat-resistant will burn and bubble off. A primer coat usually isn't necessary with these special paints; two undiluted, full-strength coats, painted on with a brush or applied with a sprayer, should be sufficient.

3 For pipes and radiators, solvent-based paints are best; most water-based paints will discolor when heated.

DOOR AND WINDOW HARDWARE

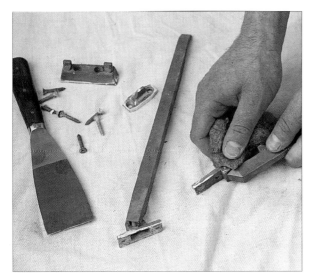

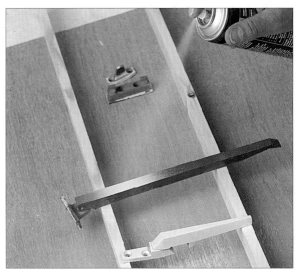

1 Tarnish and spots of paint can be cleaned off most window hardware with fine-grade steel wool. However, this method may scratch or abrade some surfaces, so try a small test area first. As an alternative, you also could use the edge of a scraper to remove the old paint.

2 Some window hardware can be rejuvenated or blended into your new color scheme by being sprayed with aerosol paint. Make sure that the paint is suitable for the hardware's type of metal, and support the items on a couple of wooden battens to provide access to all sides when spraying.

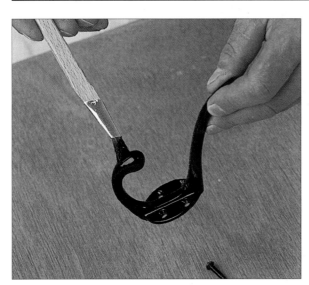

3 Or, paint hardware using a small fitch brush. Put them on clean cardboard so they won't stick to your drop cloths as they dry.

4 Don't paint the screws before reattaching the hardware; a screwdriver will just mar the paint. Simply touch up the screws when they're replaced.

Floors

Painting a concrete floor is an inexpensive way to clean up and give color to what would otherwise be a dull, dusty surface. A new concrete floor should be allowed to cure and dry out for up to six months before painting.

Wooden flooring can be split into two broad categories: blocks and planks. Both types need to be sealed to provide a practical, usable surface. Although there's a wide variety of finishes available, all wooden floors are prepared in much the same way.

TOOLS: Broom, 4-inch paintbrush, paint bucket, hammer, nail set, floor sander, floor polisher

MATERIALS: Cement mix, clean cloth, solvent, floor paint, wax/oil/varnish

CONCRETE FLOORS

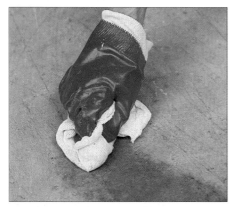

1 Sweep the concrete floor with a soft brush to remove all dirt and debris. Fill any cracks or holes with a cement mix and allow them to dry. Wipe the floor with a damp cloth to make sure it's dust-free. Oil and grease marks should be removed using a solvent or grease remover. If there's no baseboard, overlap the wall paint onto the floor by approximately 2 inches to make it easier to achieve a neat, straight line at the edges with the floor paint.

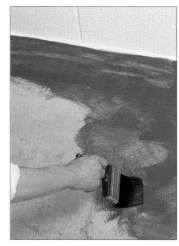

2 Remember to open all windows and doors to provide good ventilation, get rid of potentially harmful paint fumes, and speed drying. Thin the first coat of the floor paint with the recommended solvent, carefully following the manufacturer's instructions. Thinning allows the paint to soak into the concrete, sealing the surface. Always work from a corner toward the door.

3 Allow the first, thinned coat of paint to dry thoroughly. Then apply two more coats of undiluted floor paint. While the floor is drying, it will be tacky and will mark easily, so keep doors shut to prevent children and pets from straying onto the newly painted surface.

WOODEN FLOORS

1 Use a nail set to sink protruding nails, and fix any loose boards. Always start a sander tilted back to avoid damaging the floor while the sander isn't moving. Sand along the grain, starting with a coarse grade of paper and finishing with a fine grade. On old floors, be sure to remove all traces of previous finishes to get a sound base on which to apply your new treatment.

USING AN INDUSTRIAL SANDER

Large industrial sanders are reasonably inexpensive to rent and save a lot of time when sanding a wooden floor. However, they're extremely noisy and dusty; ear protection, goggles, and a dust mask are musts. Open all windows to maximize ventilation, and consider sealing all inside doors with masking tape to keep sanding dust out of the rest of the house.

A large sander won't be able to get within about 2 inches of a wall. Once you've sanded the main part of the floor, you'll have to go back and finish the edges with a smaller, hand-held power sander.

2 Vacuum the area to free it of dust, wipe the floor using a cloth dampened with solvent, and allow it to dry. A sealing coat then can be applied. As shown here, wax should be worked well into the grain using a lint-free cloth.

3 Once the wax has dried, use an electric floor polisher to buff the surface. Keep applying coats until a deep sheen is achieved. A natural wax floor may need many applications in order to achieve the desired effect, but it will improve as the finish ages.

Staining and varnishing

These sealing coats are designed both to protect bare wood and to enhance its natural grain and pattern. However, because they're translucent, any small defects in the wood will show through the final finish. Therefore, before applying any type of stain or varnish, take extra time to check that every surface has been prepared thoroughly and that all marks or traces of previous paint have been completely removed.

Work without stopping, if at all possible, because keeping a wet edge is important to avoid unsightly brush marks.

TOOLS: Varnish brushes, paint bucket

MATERIALS: Varnish, wood stain, solvent, sandpaper, clean cloth

STAINING

1 Staining tends to result in more dramatic coloring than varnishing and is ideal to blend different types of wood together. When staining a door, use the same order of work as for painting (see pages 74–75). Be careful not to overlap sections or allow drips to occur—they'll show in the final finish. Because of this, it's always best to work with the door supported on a flat surface, making sure that the underside is adequately padded to prevent damage.

2 Brush the stain well into the grain, checking often that no surface buildup has occurred. Then apply subsequent coats of stain to increase the durability of the finish or, if you like, simply to build up the depth of color in the wood.

VARNISHING

1 When using solvent-based varnish on bare wood, the first coat should be thinned (use 10 parts varnish to 1 part solvent) and used as a primer/sealer. Apply it with a lint-free cloth, rubbing well into, and in the direction of, the grain. Acrylic varnishes can be brushed on undiluted and without thinning.

2 Allow the varnish to dry, and use fine-grade sandpaper to gently smooth the surface, removing any dust or grit. Wipe the surface clean using a cloth dampened with solvent.

3 Use a clean brush to apply the next coat of varnish. Don't overload the brush, and use even strokes to brush the varnish well into the grain. Several coats will be needed for a long-lasting finish. Lightly sand and wipe clean between coats.

3 Treat the vertical stiles and the horizontal members of a paneled door as though they were separate parts, making clean straight lines at their joints with the stain. This will prevent brush marks in the wrong direction from showing on either area and ruining the clean look of the wood grain.

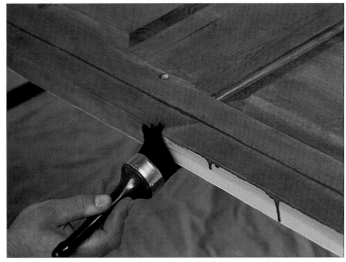

4 Drips are sometimes unavoidable. Deal with them quickly before they dry. Check for drips often during the drying process, and brush them away immediately.

SEPARATE BRUSHES
Brushes used for paint can bleed color, muddying a clear varnished finish. That's why it's always a good idea to keep separate inventories of varnish and painting brushes.

Waxing and oiling

Wood is fed and nourished by waxes and oils. They prevent it from drying out and cracking—a common problem in modern homes—and provide a different feel and texture than the more common sealing stains and varnishes, not to mention their beauty.

Oil is a particularly good finish for hardwoods such as oak and ash, and it even will revive the most faded, worn areas, restoring them to their former glory. On bare wood, two coats of wax are adequate, but additional coats will build up depth of color and sheen.

For more information on applying waxes and oils, see page 15.

TOOLS: 1- and 1½-inch paintbrushes, paint bucket

MATERIALS: Sandpaper, oil, lint-free cloth, wax, dye

OILING

2 After a few minutes, use a lint-free cloth to wipe off any surplus oil that hasn't soaked into the wood. Areas that are subjected to heavy wear, such as floors, may need several applications of the oil.

1 Prepare the bare wood as usual (see pages 32–33), and apply the oil sparingly, using a brush or cloth.

FIRE RISK
Old oil-soaked cloths and rags are highly flammable. After use, soak them in water and seal them in an old paint can to be disposed of safely.

WAXING

1 Thoroughly sand all surfaces, working along the grain where possible. In more intricate areas, such as the moldings of a stair rail as shown here, it may be easier to roll the sandpaper into a tube. Dust the area and wipe it off with a cloth dampened with solvent.

2 Apply the wax with a lint-free cloth, working it along the grain of the wood. Don't worry too much about getting a completely streak-free finish; any unattractive marks or buildup of the wax will soon disappear when the surface is buffed and polished.

3 For areas of fine detail, a cloth isn't always the best tool for the job. Use a small brush to get into these awkward areas.

COLOR CHECKS

Most waxes contain their own pigmentation, so it's wise to test a small area in an inconspicuous spot before waxing the entire surface. Using a wood dye before applying the wax is another way to color the wood; apply it with a brush or cloth. Most wood dyes can be mixed with each other, allowing you many choices of color. Again, test a small area to check the color.

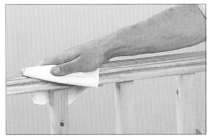

4 After approximately 15 minutes, buff the waxed areas with a soft clean cloth, again working along the wood grain wherever possible. Fine-grade steel wool also may be used for this purpose. Apply additional coats using the same technique.

Problems and mistakes

All kinds of problems and mistakes happen during painting—or after you're done painting. Most of them can be written off to poor preparation, incompatible paints, rushed work, or just sloppy application. So always remember to read the manufacturer's directions for each specific coating, and never try to cut corners. Some problems can be fixed more easily than others. The most common ones are shown here.

POOR COVERAGE

Usually found where a solvent-based gloss has been applied over the wrong undercoat, or even no undercoat at all. Sand the surface down and reapply the correct paint. With water-based paints, it's usually due to insufficient coverage. Adding extra coats usually will solve the problem.

MISCELLANEOUS STAINS

Damp patches and rust spots are most often found with water-based paints because solvent-based finishes usually will cover up problems like these. Apply a stain block, allow it to dry, and repaint the surface. For persistent damp stains or unidentifiable marks, consult a professional.

ROLLER TRAILS

These occur in uneven areas because the roller is unable to run across the surface smoothly. They also are caused by applying too much pressure to the roller while it's moving. Lightly sand and repaint the area.

ORANGE PEEL/WRINKLING

Caused when a solvent-based paint is applied over a first coat of paint that hasn't had time to dry completely. Strip the paint back to the bare surface and repaint, this time allowing adequate drying time between coats.

DRIPS AND RUNS

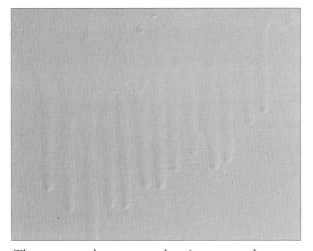

These occur when too much paint was used on a vertical surface. Allow the paint to dry completely, sand the area to remove the runs and to achieve a smooth surface, then repaint.

GRIT OR DIRT

Caused either by poor initial preparation of surfaces or by dirt that was picked up by the brush during painting. Lightly sand the area, wipe it clean with a dampened cloth, and repaint.

BRUSH MARKS

Caused by general overapplication of paint or lack of evening out or laying off. Usually worse with wood stain. To solve the problem for both paint and wood stain, sand the area or, in severe cases, strip it completely. Then reapply the paint or wood stain.

BLISTERING/BUBBLING

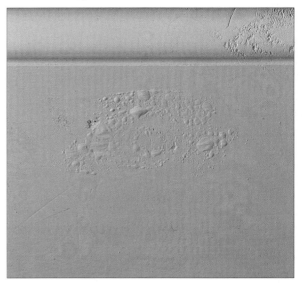

Occurs when moisture or air is trapped beneath the paint and expands due to heat. Strip the area to bare wood, fill any holes, and repaint. Similar-looking bubbles also occur with water-based paints on plaster. They're from poor preparation or dusty surfaces. Sand, prep the surface, and repaint.

Cleanup and storage

When your painting is done, always thoroughly clean your equipment before putting it away. Don't make the common mistake of leaving brushes in a jar of solvent, expecting them to be as good as new in six months' time; they'll simply dry out and you'll have to throw them away. Taking good care of your expensive brushes and rollers can save you money. Although cleaning up may seem like extra trouble and work, you'll be glad you did it when you start your next painting project.

Remember to safely dispose of any empty paint cans or leftover chemicals.

TOOLS: Scraper, crafts knife

MATERIALS: Household detergent, steel wool, solvent, glass jar, clean cloth, brown paper, rubber band, hand cleaner

WATER-BASED PAINT

2 Wash out brushes using the same technique for rollers or pads. To remove any dried paint, draw a dull scraper across the bristles. Steel wool is handy for cleaning up ferrules or metal roller cages that have become caked with dried paint.

1 Clean rollers or pads by first wiping off excess paint on old newspaper. Then wash the pad or roller cover under running water until the water runs clear. Better yet, use a mild household detergent that's safe for your equipment. Rinse and shake dry.

CLEANING HANDS

Many paints and finishes irritate the skin, so it's best to wear gloves. Still, the occasional splash of paint is unavoidable. To clean hands, use soap and water for latex paints; for solvent-based paints, use a solvent, then wash with soap and water.

SOLVENT-BASED PAINT

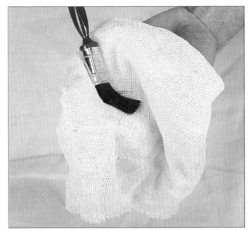

2 Take the brush out, removing the excess liquid by drawing the bristles across the edge of the jar. Dry the brush thoroughly with a clean cloth. Repeat Steps 1 and 2 if paint is still evident in the bristles. Finally, wash the brush with warm water and detergent, then rinse it and shake it dry.

1 Remove excess paint from the brush and stir the brush vigorously in a jar of solvent or commercial brush cleaner.

PROFESSIONAL BRUSH KEEPER

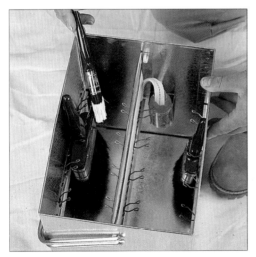

On big painting jobs that span several days, you may feel as if you do as much brush cleaning as you do painting, especially when using solvent-based paints. That's why professional painters sometimes use a box like this to keep several same-color brushes moist and ready to reuse without having to thoroughly clean them at the end of each day.

REMOVING PAINT FROM CARPET

When your work is done and the room is returned to normal, it's not uncommon to find that paint has somehow managed to find its way through the drop cloths and onto your carpet. Once the paint has dried out, small spots can be removed with a sharp crafts knife. Don't cut down—just carefully scrape the carpet fibers across the surface of the carpet. You'll be amazed at how this simple technique makes the paint disappear.

STORAGE

All brushes should be dry before you put them away. To keep them in like-new condition, wrap the bristles in brown paper held in place with a rubber band. This will help the brush keep its shape so the bristles won't splay out in all directions.

Glossary

Beading
Using the very edge of a paintbrush to make a precise dividing line between two colors.

Butt joint
A joint where two edges of wallpaper or lining paper meet but do not overlap.

Casement window
A window made up of hinged and/or fixed lights (glass panes).

Ceiling fixture
An electrical fixture found on ceilings through which a lighting pendant hangs.

Cutting in
Painting into a corner, such as between a wall and ceiling, or onto a narrow surface, such as on a sash window.

Double lining
Two layers of lining paper used to achieve a smooth finish on a rough surface.

Feathering
Blending in uneven edges during sanding.

Ferrule
The metal band on a paintbrush that holds the bristles onto the handle.

Flush
The term used to describe two level, adjacent surfaces.

Fungicide
A chemical that kills mold.

Laying off
Light brush strokes in the same direction used to eliminate brush marks left on a painted surface.

Lining paper
Plain paper that provides a smooth surface on walls and ceilings before painting or hanging wall coverings.

Lint-free cloth
A cloth, usually made of cotton, that does not shed its fibers.

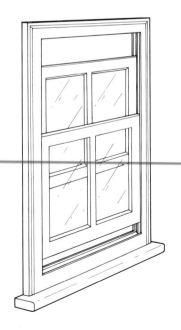

Lumber
A length of straight wood, often used as a guideline.

Members
Horizontal wooden components that are part of a paneled door.

Overlapping butt joint
The process of overlapping wall coverings, cutting through both layers of paper, and removing the excess strips to create a flush butt joint.

Primer
Thinned, specially formulated paint that seals and stabilizes a surface before painting.

Rails
The horizontal and vertical components of a window.

Rebate
The part of a rail that's at a right angle to the pane of glass.

Recessed window
A window that's flush with the outside wall, making a recess inside the room.

Sash window
A window in which the opening sections, or the sashes, slide up and down inside a frame, counterbalanced by weights held on sash cords.

Size
A stabilizing compound applied to porous surfaces to seal them before hanging wallpaper.

Stiles
Vertical components that are part of a paneled door.

Tooth
A slightly rough surface that's been sanded to provide a better bond for paint or wallpaper.

Index

Meredith® Press
An imprint of Meredith® Books

Do-It-Yourself Decorating
Step-by-Step Interior Painting
Editor, Shelter Books: Denise L. Caringer
Contributing Editor: David A. Kirchner
Contributing Designer: Jeff Harrison
Copy Chief: Angela K. Renkoski

Meredith® Books
Editor in Chief: James D. Blume
Managing Editor: Christopher Cavanaugh
Director, New Product Development: Ray Wolf
Vice President, Retail Sales: Jamie L. Martin

Meredith Publishing Group
President, Publishing Group: Christopher M. Little
Vice President and Publishing Director: John P. Loughlin

Meredith Corporation
Chairman of the Board and Chief Executive Officer: Jack D. Rehm
President and Chief Operating Officer: William T. Kerr
Chairman of the Executive Committee: E. T. Meredith III

First published 1996 by Haynes Publishing

All of us at Meredith® Books are dedicated to providing you with information and ideas you need to enhance your home. We welcome your comments and suggestions about this book on stenciling. Write to us at: Meredith® Books, Do-It-Yourself Editorial Department, RW-206, 1716 Locust St., Des Moines, IA 50309-3023.

This edition published by Meredith Corporation, Des Moines Iowa, 1997
Printed in France
Printing Number and Year: 5 4 3 2 1 00 99 98 97 96
Library of Congress Catalog Card Number: 96-78038
ISBN: 0-696-20676-5